Merry Christmas to the Boss -

from the

"Bosses"

Claire

+ Betty

1977.

# Faces of the
# Old North

# Faces of the Old North

Cathy Wismer

McGraw-Hill Ryerson Limited

Toronto   Montreal   New York   London

Faces of the Old North

ISBN 0-07-077774-8

1 2 3 4 5 6 7 8 9 10   D   3 2 1 0 9 8 7 6 5 4

Printed and Bound in Canada

# Contents

# Preface

An angry Indian once told me to mind my own culture. I was hurt by his bluntness, but his advice made me want to take a harder look at my own cultural background.

The result was a trip into the backwoods of Northern Ontario, where I discovered not just a few thousand miles of Canada but a heritage, people who have resisted the white man's inventions as much as the natives have. These are the old trappers, miners, guides and railroad men, the bush people, living on the edges of small Northern Ontario towns.

I listened to their stories in one-room shacks and I heard a history that only the Indians and the French chansonniers had spoken of. Some of the stories had never been told. In most cases there had never been anyone there to listen. They were afraid their stories would die with them, their only permanence a shoebox full of yellow photographs.

It is with great hesitation I offer this book for publication, for I've learned to love these people, to love the very fact of their existence, knowing they are real human beings, not characters of someone's imagination.

I feel deeply my responsibility to present them as they are. They have created their own lives and legends; and the truth of their stories, their self-images, I leave for you to decide.

The photographs were taken during our conversations and the stories were taped, transcribed and put in some semblance of order.

Necessity demands that these stories be told, for they are our legacy, a small but rich inheritance from Northern Ontario. The legends and faces of the old north must now be recorded, for the men and women who created them are dying.

CATHY WISMER

*And if you could tough it,*
*you was tough. And if you*
*couldn't tough it, well,*
*you passed away.*

Lorne Saunders

# The Violinist and the Accordion Player

Gogama is a flat, dry little town where the summer trains never stop. The main street is empty at noon and the dogs lie, belly-flat, on sidewalks under pepsi-cola signs, hanging out from clapboard fronts of stores with tar-paper sides. There's one restaurant that serves Southern Fried Chicken in a basket, and the bar in the hotel is lazy, slow in putting down the midday draft.

I'd been caught in Gogama for some of the day and all of the night, with nothing but bush a hundred miles in every direction. I paid in advance my five dollars for a hotel bed, washed and settled for sleep. People back in West Shining Tree had warned me it was a frontier town, booze-crazy after dark, so I stuck to the bed, uneasy somehow, just lying there, listening to the comings and goings. My room was at the top of the stairs and the bed was next to the washroom wall, and I could hear the heavy feet coming up from the bar below, doors slamming shut somewhere down the hall.

The taps closed down at one, so the drinkers had to move outside into the night, stumbling blind, and I could hear the snap of fists finding a jawbone, a curse and tires scorching the asphalt which runs the half-mile to the highway. The backwood's silence was shattered again by the blast of a train as it ripped through town, twenty yards from the hotel, the first of four summer trains that night.

I didn't sleep well in Gogama. In another half-day, I was gone, up the highway seventeen miles to the Mattagami Reserve and this is my story about Willy Moore and Jessie Mann and how I found them in the cabin, Willy sitting by the window, his left leg dangling, half a foot shorter than the right, and Jessie, rolling the last of her tobacco into a cigarette.

11

They were shy with me at first, not saying too much, but we got over the awkwardness with a bottle of wine, Quebec red, Willy complaining it was too dry, but he'd drink it anyway. Jessie kept us filled, saluting every time with a toothless grin, no question of seconds or thirds, and we'd all clunk our glasses in a round of toasts. The stories started to come, slow, first Willy, remembering the time he'd tasted tea and then the summers they camped at the Hudson Bay Trading Post up the lake, tenting and eating with white traders. His mother got mixed up with a Scotsman there, married, and that's how he got the name Willy Moore. Forty percent of him, he figured, was Scottish.

Jessie interrupted, clapping a large hand to her chest, which had slipped to her waist over the years. "Me all Indian. Ojibway. Still strong woman. Carry canoe two miles on back. Maybe eighty years now."

You could tell she had always been six inches taller than her old friend Willy, big-boned and broad in the back. And when she moved it was like some flatfooted animal, stretching on hind quarters. But you couldn't go after the stories with Jessie. She was Indian enough to keep them to herself, at least until you proved a friend.

In the past hour, we'd gathered quite an audience in the little cabin. I'd watched them through the window, coming in twos and threes across the field, some now inside, leaning against the wall, others squatting on the doorstep. The chief, his brother, his brother-in-law, his wife and her children and their friends, about thirty in all, crowding and listening. A couple of heads twisted in pin curls peered over buckskin shoulders, all eyes were black and curious.

Jessie disappeared into the back room, bringing out Willy's cedar fiddle, the one he'd made. And how it all happened, I'm still not sure, but Jessie got started on the accordion, some Gaelic tune, and Willy picked up the fiddle, working it like a crossbow on his knee, and the dancing began. And I guess what I remember most is Jessie, her eyes half-shut, my last cigarette stuck in the side of her mouth, smiling and squeezing out the music, and Willy, tilting in the chair, pressing the cat strings, his good leg tapping the floor a full note behind everyone else.

It was too good a time to leave, but I was bunking down in Timmins and that was another two hours away. Jessie padded me over to the door, grabbed my arm and left me with a wet kiss. Her name for me was Wahbishewa. She'd called me White Woman. Perhaps next time there'd be stories.

# Abie Booth

I met a fellow whose grandfather had told him about Grey Owl's wedding—a big boozing party on the steamboat *Belle*, floating for a day out of Temagami. I found his grandfather, Abie Booth, back in the bush at the end of a trapline which twisted in 24 miles from the highway, on the north side of Marten River. That's how I got to be sitting down with Abie in his cabin, the logs notched and squared by his own hands, and outside, tacked on the door, a fistful of notes telling where he had gone if he wasn't answering.

But there's no doubt about it," Abie was saying, "this here Grey Owl, that's Archie Delaney, did save the beaver. Breeding them and writing books about it. But he was a bigamist and it was only his messing around with other Indian women after marrying old Angel on the *Belle* that turned the town sour."

Abie wouldn't talk about Archie unless he was asked. The way he figured, it was mostly the injustice of it, Archie writing all those books, making himself a hero, presenting the Ojibways' grievances in front of the King, when he was just as English as the ground he stood on. There's lots of characters more deserving, though they never got into books.

And to tell the truth, he said, he was glad I'd come. Reckoned he had all the material for someone to write a real book. Abie took a deep breath, his chest rising a little under the tartan shirt, and said it wasn't just for bragging but he was the original guy who named the Polar Bear Express. That's the train that goes up the Moosonee Line and he was there on its first run out of Temagami, chalking up the name on the engine hood. That was his bit of work, naming the Polar Bear, though not many knew it.

He'd taken off his Aussie hat, being the gentleman he was, and he pulled at the leopard band, his talk dying fast, fading to half-sentences, then silence. He'd gone shy, worried in case his stories weren't good enough, weighing them too hard against Archie's. Doubting his own history, the very stuff he wanted to share. But he gave in to persuasion and said he had a story, how it really were, and his hand started working like a Frenchman's, showing the way old Johnny Cariboo's moustache was turned up as if he'd swallowed a horse and couldn't get the tail down, the night they'd been in the boozer. Abie was saying he got drunk enough to tell old Johnny he was setting up a guiding camp and old Johnny had been sober enough to tell Abie it was pure Tonomo. That's b.s. in Ojibway, if you know what b.s. means. And that's how the camp got its name and how it come to be.

He laughed, dropping a small fist hard as a bullet on the table, and oh my god, he'd had Americans name their racehorse after it, never knowing. Got a picture of the horse in his biscuit tin and lots more photos too, like the one of the Supreme Court judge who presided at Nuremberg, a friend he'd guided for twenty years. And there was one of his dogteam, hitched for trapping. He said he could talk to them like people, some of them almost human. But they all died and he'd been with himself since. And there was the bear he shot, with a twenty-two, a Ruga semi-automatic, when he used to hunt for a living. Swore he could knock the eye out of a snake with it. The other gun harnessed above his bunk was a jungle rifle, killed a lot of moose. Above the upper bunk was something I figured he'd forgotten company could see: his 1940s pin-up, fading yellow.

He was after me to drink some Grand Marnier and ginger ale, something he kept for occasions, and he was up, moving like a young boxer, his tiny feet laced up in trapper's boots, his jeans tucked in a pair of grey dime-store socks. He poured two fingers, apologizing for the china, and handed me a mug, sitting down on the bed with tea for himself. Used to overdose in drinking, but he gave it all up when he bloodied his nose falling over a canoe three years back.

The two of us sat drinking and watching the birds outside the cabin door dropping down and feeding off the muskrat he'd skinned the night before. Inside, the morning light was coming in at blocks and angles, squared by the open door and the window, its pattern on the table. The window ledge was stacked with cartridge boxes, Listerine, an upper set of teeth for Legion dances, soupcans of cutlery and pencils, a mayonnaise jar of nuts and screws and an old buglehorn once used to blast the troops out of their beds.

You could tell Abie was thinking of his next story, his eyes transparent, his mouth half moving, rehearsing his opening. He was off somewhere up his trapline.

There's times I'd get caught on the line, dig a hole in the snow, be about five feet, put cut brush in and bed down, then build the fire up against a fallen root, put a blanket up with sticks for a windbreak and get in with the dogs. They'd snuggle right up with you.

I still trap and read when I'm not trappin'. A terrific reader, self-educatin' though. I'm putrid at grammar and spellin'. I've got no diaries, never bothered with 'em. I can remember things back when I was one year old and I was in petticoats. And I can remember in London when we were livin' there when we was just youngsters, urchins, and when there was only horse-drawn street cars.

I was always tops in all classes. Sketchin' and drawin'. And when we moved back up to Bradford, I went to school there. The school was in a little village four miles away. Oakenstrand. That's where that Ann Sucksmith was. That was in Yorkshire and there's a lot of country there and we lived like all our parents, come from small out-villages.

My grandfather, the one I'm called after, used to have a tavern and horses. He used to breed horses, carriage horses and huntin' horses for the gents. So I was always in the country and when I was goin' to school I had that teacher, Miss Sucksmith, Ann Sucksmith. I guess I got to be a favorite of hers. I loved botany, pickin' flowers, and she used to give prizes and I used to win them all. Gatherin' up flowers every weekend and goin' back to school Monday and the one what got the most wild, different flowers she'd give them a prize. Well hell, I used to beat them all, hands down. I used to collect birds' eggs for her and I'd birdwatch and find the bird's nest and take one or two eggs and blow 'em and take 'em to her, and she'd put them all in a little bowl in a little museum.

I worshipped that woman, someway or another. I don't know why. I really liked 'er 'cause she used to take an interest in me and I could learn more off her than I could in a thousand classes.

Like talkin' bout opportunities. I don't want you to think I'm braggin', I'm only tellin' you this 'cause I'm more or less just lonesome and just openin' up, not braggin'.

We soon moved from the village to Bradford. That's when I started fulltime workin' in the mill. I'm walkin' down the street and I'd just come from work. I had my white smock on (we all had our white smocks on), little jumpers goin' down the street, and I saw this great big car. There wasn't too many cars in those days. I'd be about fourteen, I guess. Anyway, this woman and her husband were real gentry. They stopped me and accosted me and asked where I lived. And I wondered what in hell I'd done wrong again, what with this man and woman comin' out of this big car. I said, "I'm Abie Booth."

"Do you live far? Can we see your parents? Will you take us to your parents?" I didn't know what they wanted. So I took them home, about half a block to walk. Mother was home; Dad wasn't home from work yet. I took them in and they made themselves acquainted, more or less. They'd been sent from the School Board of Education in London and they'd traced me right up, through my sketches and drawings, schoolwork I did in London. And the school had sent them up to get a hold of me and they wanted to take me back to London and put me through the School of Academy and pay for everything and it wouldn't have cost me a nickel or nothin'.

Well, Dad come home just a little later on and they said they'd call in again the next day, you know, and if the bags was ready they'd take me. Well, Dad asked me and I said no, I didn't want to go back to London. He said it was up to me.

We were not in too good standin', there was ten of a family, and I was a big shot 'cause I was workin'. I got one shillin' and elevenpence halfpenny for the week, workin' from six o'clock in the mornin' 'til noon. Saturdays too. And now, that's the gospel truth. Talk about child labor. But I was proud takin' home one shillin'. Just shows you. I turned that down. I can see the foolishness, the opportunity. I used to love paintin' and interior decoratin' and flowers, but I got right off of it and I won't even pick up a pencil now. I was a fool to let it go. I'd 'ave gone in for portrait, right into detail, especially in oils. It just seemed to come to me natural.


I joined up for the first World War when I was sixteen, in France and Belgium, and then I ended up in Russia and that big fight there at the Somme. Bully Court was where I got taken prisoner of war, in Germany. There was that big push and we were on the Somme front, spearheaded, with French on the right and Portuguese on the other side. We had a terrific shelling there.

We got orders from headquarters, which was Sir Marshall Folkes then, he was the head commander and he sent word through to hold the line at all costs, don't retreat. That was the 59th Division I was in. We had to spread out and hold the line and we got orders not to retreat. The outfit that I was with when I got caught, taken prisoner, was the Second Six Sherwood Foresters. And at the end of the war I got a letter from Sir Marshall Folkes in Cochrane. Only six of us returned out of the whole division of men.

I was in several camps. They kept us behind the lines on reprisals. I was missin' for nine months before they knew at home. I was presumed dead. They drew my insurance even, for godsake's.

Wicked, those camps. People can't really realize them prisoner of war camps. The worst place I was in was a place called Schneidermuell. I got sent to this Schneidermuell, that's up in the corridor on the Polish border between Russia and Germany and Poland.

But I was lucky that I happened to hit what I did there, when I got taken prisoner. I was a sniper. If you happen to be taken prisoner you're supposed to destroy your paybook 'cause it's marked in, you see. We snipers got an extra shillin' a day. If ever the enemy sees the book and finds out they'll shoot you right there. Show no mercy. So I destroyed my paybook. I was just taken as an ordinary prisoner. I don't know where everybody got to, but I was the only one left that day I got taken. We was on a sunken road and we were holdin' this sunken road on a place called 'ickory Corner. When the Germans came in, I had nothing left, I didn't even have a bullet. All I had was my rifle and bayonet.

I was so goddamn young, I guess. I can never forget, they were comin' over four abreast. I'd been firin' up to my last, but I could see 'em comin' up this road and I was snipin' them off. Anyway, I had nothing left. There was four or five of 'em jumped down off the top of the trench and one of them was hittin' me on top of the bloody head with one of them 'tater mashers, we called them. That's a German bomb like a tin milk can with a handle on it. And I had my rifle and I guess he was tryin' to tell me to drop it. Surrender. But I didn't know what the hell he was talkin' about. And there was all the others and one was shovin' a revolver in my guts 'til finally my gun was knocked out of my hands. I got taken back behind the lines for months. They were usin' us to carry up ammunition and to carry wounded back on reprisals.

We were kept in barb-wire pens and nobody knew where I was,

only that I was in that engagement and I was missin', possibly wounded and then presumed dead. That's when I got sent up to Schneidermuell Camp. Wicked. You starved to death and you worked to death. It was all sand in the camp, white sand, pretty close up to the seacoast right on the corridor on the Baltic Sea. All sand in the compound and you'd sink into it and they'd tie us all together and double us around in the sand 'til we all dropped. This German would be on a pony, on that goddamned pony, with a big strong whip. People can't realize it.

It just got to be I didn't give a damn what happened, whether I got killed or anything. That's the reason why I volunteered to go out on these working parties from the camp and I used to sabotage like hell every goddarn thing I could.

After this here Schneidermuell, we got sent to a village called Kreuzavich where I had to work for an old guy, we called him Brudgel, but his name was Jonathan Knoscki. He had a Polish name but he was a real Nazi. He used to hate our guts. In fact, once he shot at me with a revolver. He tried to kill me. If it hadn't been for his daughter Vera, he would have done. She was workin' with us in the mill; she used to do all the bookkeeping. The Gestapo used to come in and take inventory. I started to learn her English and she started to learn me how to speak German.

But this one time, I was upstairs in the flour mill with the worm screws (they weren't workin') and Brudgel had given me this damned old hammer and the head kept fallin' off. You couldn't work with it and I told him, but he wouldn't give me another. So I'd have to climb down right from up above everytime I threw the hammer head off. Down to the cellar everytime, up and down, up and down. I done that two or three times before I asked him again and "Enklish schweinhund," he yells, "zum Teufel, nochmal." That means what the hell. That was good enough for me. So I tell him to go to hell. Well, jesus, the hammer came off again and I sat down and wouldn't come down, and he's yellin', "Kommen herunter, gefetchen." I didn't move. He got so mad and he used to be one of those guys that took epileptic fits, foam at the mouth. He took off and said he was goin' to shoot me. I knew somethin' was goin' to happen, so I came down to the second floor. You see, the house and the mill and stable were all combined. That's when Vera came in and asked what's the matter.

The old man came back up the stairs, two at a time, a great big long guy, six-foot-four, and he had a gun. I stood right 'longside the window. I couldn't understand him half, he was spittin' the words. And he out with the gun and Vera saw it and she screamed and she got hold of him, bit him, but he fired it and missed me. If it hadn't been for her . . .

At the mill I got to know a young Polish boy, through speakin' German, and they hated the Germans. I used to steal flour out of the mill for him and he'd give it to his mother and his mother used to make cakes to feed the others. She made me a canvas bag with a belt and I could fill it up with flour without being too conspicuous. I'd steal the flour and hide it out in the yard and he'd come at night and get it and take it home. He'd sometimes leave some of his mother's cakes. That's the way we used to exchange. I could always provide myself with enough food there, because we used to steal a lot.

I used to go in and kill pigeons what was hangin' around in the yard and I got to be a past master at it. We called them Toba, the pigeons. We got caught one day though. We made a raid up in the loft and I got this Billy Stone to go in where there was two bob holes cut out, and we took a gunny sack and cleaned out the whole brood. But one of them pigeons was standin' right in the bob hole and Billy made a grab for it. If you grab hold of a pigeon's tail, the tail will come out in your hand and the bird will fly away. And that's what happened. Billy missed it.

Well, we were livin' up in the top storey, right up in the garret (that's where they kept the prisoners) and there was a garret window and we could see down in the yard. The next morning, the old lady, Brudgel's wife, was there. She used to come and throw the wheat out and whistle for the pigeons, but that morning there was only this goddamn one pigeon that came down from the roofs and she called her husband, let me see if I can interpret it. She called the old man "Eine tobe—ich gehaben keine schwanz"—there's only one pigeon and he hasn't got no tail.

We laughed. They never did find out. We was killin' them and givin' them to young Ignace. The Polish people what was around lived across the road, there's maybe about ten families livin' in one house. They all kept nanny goats. I know, 'cause when we escaped I killed one in a field and that's what we fed on, and if it hadn't been for that there old nanny goat, we would never have made it. We ate it raw. You daren't build fires.

Half the time at the mill, Brudgel's, I sabotaged the boilers. I cut the water off the main valve and the first thing I know all the damn pipes inside are shrivelled up and leaking, and they'd have to put in new pipes and I'd hold them up for weeks at a time. They couldn't mill no corn or anything. There was the sugar factory too, with sixty prisoners working there. The way they make the sugar there is with big turnips, sugar beets. The Germans made all their explosives, glycerine, out of sugar for wartime. We set fire to the damn place twice.

Brudgel had another daughter, I just forget her name. This one what bit him was Vera, but there was this younger daughter, a teenage girl, she wasn't much younger than I was. After the war was finished in '18 I was only nineteen. Possibly she was about sixteen, a beautiful lookin' girl and I got along good with her.

The older daughter, Vera, what was married, had a little girl and a husband named Rudolphe Schlucks, a Landern Profiteer Engross. That means he's like a buyer, a purchasin' agent for the army. But he used to come home now and then. He was like an Anglo-Saxon fellow. He was a prince of a fellow. When things was gettin' so bad towards the end, when the war got real bad, he heard that the old man Brudgel was goin' to lose the mill, they were goin' to confiscate everything with the English army and give it all back to the Polish people again.

He asked me if I'd like to go and stay at his place 'til we see how things come out. So I said sure and he took me. He had a reason too. I saved his wife's life. Right in her father's place. A big German mastiff dog had her down on the floor and it could have killed her. I killed the dog.

He took me over to his house. They lived just on the outskirts of the village. It was like a big wall all around it, with broken glass on top and big gates. It was one of them great big dome places, you seen these here domes on Russian and Polish places. He was a millionaire. He used to go to all the farmers and estimate all the crops for the Germans. In peacetime he'd go to the docks and buy freight, whole cargoes, and put them on the stocks.

It was 'im I ended up with near the end of the war. Old Brudgel closed the mill down. We stole eight or nine big bags of flour and took them up to Rudolphe's house unknown to the Gestapo, and we hid them in this place, enough to last them twelve months or more. We got along and their little girl used to go crazy when I brought out my slate and drew dogs and cats and cows.

And there was a German girl who was a teacher who'd stay with us on weekends. She was a very refined girl. On Sundays she'd invite me down for coffee. It was burnt barley (that's all they had for coffee). They used to keep a coffee pot goin' on the stove steady. This teacher

came in and sat down and I was makin' a sketch of her. I was measurin' her, makin' a rough sketch. Just once I could see she knew what I was doin'. After a while she came over and looked at it, and asked me if I could finish it. Just before the war was over she begged me to go to Berlin after the war. She wanted me to stay there, in fact, I think she wanted me to marry her! I was too patriotic. (Rudolphe wanted me to stay, too. When I did leave he gave me a thousand-mark note.) This girl even wanted to put me through the art school in Berlin. There was another chance I missed.


I guess Vera and I got to be good friends at the mill, what with me killin' that dog and she savin' my life. Before I moved to her and Rudolphe's place, she started makin' sure I got those packages from Geneva. The first ones I'd ever got. Eight-pound packages from neutral countries was supposed to come every seven days, if you were lucky. Packaged food, soap, for the prisoners of war. Now soap in Germany during the war was the main item. You could go and if you knew the proper way you could almost buy a whole village with a bar of soap. It was that valuable.

I'd once busted out of camp there in Schneidermuell. I'd met a corporal there who was right from my hometown and practically lived on my street. Birdswell was his name. In the German army even a corporal is an officer, so this English fellow didn't have to work if he didn't want to. He wasn't allowed to. This here Birdswell, he never did, so I got talkin' to him. He'd won some medal, some military cross. (I don't know how the hell he ever got it—must have come up in the rations. They was the first to open them.) So I got with him and told him let's break camp. We were about three miles from the regular city. Birdswell was getting packages, I wasn't yet.

"Have you got anything in your package?" He says yes.

"What have you got?"

"Well," he says, "soap, cigarettes, cocoa, tea..."

Oh my goodness, soap was better than gold. You could bribe anyone with just a slice of soap. Not a bar. Just cut a thin slice off.

Now the guards were all around the pens. They were pretty well all old men or young boys. Anyway, we bribed them and we got out. But we didn't know who was goin' to be there when we got back, so we tried to tell them to make it known we'd give them cigarettes. We took off a couple of times. We even went to a movie show, honest to god!

These Russians, they capitulated, so they were allowed out of the camp and they could were anything—sometines they were wearing our uniforms. (The English uniform's all blue with a brown band on your arm and sometimes on your back and the Russians could wear them.) So I traded my uniform off for one of these old coats of the Russians. And I could speak enough German to get by.

We went into a tavern and had some schnapps and then I got talkin' to two of the barmaids. I told them we were English prisoners and she said, "Have you got any soap?" And I said "yah". We gave them a little piece of soap and, my god, we could get anything!

After the war finished they turned us loose and, hell, I was way up on the borders of Russia. The German army just went haywire; they threw up everything and took off home, shootin' and lootin'. After I left Rudolphe's place, it took Billy Stone and me six weeks to walk to the nearest port. He was from Leicester, and me and him got sent up together. Now we were goin' into Danzig together to get a Danish boat. These boats were goin' around different places pickin' up prisoners of war that been turned loose, 'cause you couldn't ride trains or nothin!

I came over to Canada in the spring of 1922, March 21. I can remember that 'cause that's the day I got taken prisoner. I brought my youngest sister with me. If she'd waited with the rest of the family to come, she'd have had to pay full fare. I paid her half-fare. We were eight days comin' across in a damn old packet boat and it was loaded all down in the hol' with these here Doukhobors. They looked like those pictures of gleaners, all in shawls, the way they dress. We got off at Quebec and they all came on the same train, all 'em old wooden carriages, and they were goin' out west. My sister got mixed up with some of the kids. Well, I could speak German and they could speak German and I got in there too. They had goddamn baskets with bloody chickens in them, bringin' all their worldly possessions with them. And my sister, she got so lousy, she was as lousy as a pet coon. And when we got home to my auntie's place in Cochrane, her hair was just loaded with lice, from mixing.

We made it our home there. Then we got Mother out. Between me and Dad we bought a house. Built greenhouses, forty-five feet by twenty feet, grew tomatoes and mushrooms. We even started an experimental farm in Kapuskasing.

Here's 'ow I come to meet my wife. My sister Annie and my wife used to work together in England. They were burlers and menders. After the cloth's all weaved pickin' all them knots off, and sometimes when they're weavin', if the machine is not properly workin', the bur-lers and menders weave where the holes were made. They worked to-gether. When I came back from the war and I was goin' to Australia, I had to get some pictures taken for the passport. So I'd been and done it and I happened to run into Doris, Annie's friend. Wasn't interested in her at all when she was chums, but she asked for a picture of me before I left.

I went to Canada instead and when it got to be that we were send-ing for the family, here Doris was comin' over for a three-month visit with my sister Annie. We met them at the train and she came to stay with us in Cochrane.

And oh, the goddamn phone was ringin' every five minutes. She was very attractive. Guys wanting to date her up. More or less I started goin' around with her to take her to the odd show, more or less to protect her from all these wolves and cowboys, so that's how it came about. Poor Doris. We finally got engaged. I didn't want to get mar-ried, it was my last thoughts. But she wanted to, so holy godfather. She didn't go back to England and she stayed and got working, so we got married.

We were only married no more than three months and then her mother came over. The mother sold out over in England and came to stay with us. She sold all her furniture and every goddamn thing and moved in with us. I even gave up my bed for her. I had to make another place and she slept with my wife and I had to sleep in a single bed myself, makin' tears in that bed all the time she was there. I don't think anybody could blame me. I settled down then, more or less. I went back to work for the TNO railway and it looked to me as there was goin' to be no commotion.

When I took the job, I took the one of car cleaner. I was figurin' on gettin' to be an inspector, okayin' the cars. But the job never come up. To make extra money I opened up the barn and started repairing shoes. I could do two and three pair of shoes a night for $1.50 and I was doin' real good. I went down to the house and painted my own sign "Expert Shoe Repairer, Bulldog Soles" (that was the kinda leather, green leather) and I said "Wears like a pig's nose".

And I started up shoe repairin'. And by god, I was in full swing when her mother came over, making shoes, taking custom jobs. I got a Goodyear stitcher and I was right in business. I had all of Cochrane—had to hire another man who was workin' on the railway in his spare time. Me and him used to do a lot of fishin' together—my downfall, I guess, I used to like to go fishin'. The old mother-in-law didn't like that and she was goin' to fire this guy. The workshop and the house was together and she said when he comes back from dinner I'm goin' to tell him he's not wanted. "Look," I says to Doris, "I don't care what you and your mother do in the house, but that workshop is my business. I'll do the hirin' and the firin'." Oh, quite a row. To the old lady, I says, "You're welcome here. I've never said a wrong word to you. The cash box is right there. You can help yourself. But don't bother me over my conceptions." The old lady walked out.

Anyway, I worked all afternoon, and when I came in at suppertime, the old lady came over and apologized. So everything was all right until she started to work on Doris underneath. The old mother went to see the doctor and the doctor told her she wouldn't be able to stand the rigors of winter, so she went to book her passage and that's when she took Doris back with her. That's how it came about.

Me and Doris. I didn't want to get married. But after we got married I adored that woman, I worshipped her. It was hard. The old lady broke it up. But I never did remarry. Somewhere along the way I'd lost all faith in the whole thing, life. I wasn't interested and that's how it came to be.

That's when I went back into the bush.

The time this thing happened I was about eight miles from the camp. It had started to snow light in the morning (not more than two inches) and I'd planned to spend the night in my outpost, a tent, made it like an igloo, put branches over it. I had one dog with me, Brandy, my leader. (The four other dogs were back at the main cabin all chained up.) Brandy was a peculiar dog. His mother was an old English bobtail sheep dog, like you see on the pictures sometime. The father in him was a Pitbull terrier, a fightin' dog. He looked like a sandy-colored, ragged Airedale. He was the most wonderful dog I ever had.

Anyway, I'd taken my snowshoes with me and I had to break a trail to the outpost, but about eight miles away it started to snow so bad that I had to come back. It's a good job I'd taken Brandy with me, because goin' along the trail back to the cabin there was cataracts came down over my eyes and I was shut off. I was completely blind, right on the trail. It just came down like that and I could feel it comin'. Finally I was shut off. Solid brush. No trails, no nothing, only my own trail. . .

So I sat down and I thought, don't panic. It's the main thing, never panic if you can. Peoples what panic, that's where they lose out. I sat down but it made no difference. I couldn't see. So I rolled a couple of cigarettes and I was smokin'. I had to get back and I had seven miles to go.

I tied a piece of string on Brandy ahead of me and I told him for home. He was a well-trained dog. Of course, them trails wind in and out and what I had to do was this, I was very sensitive and I had to feel my way with the snowshoes. As soon as ever I got to one side, whoop, you'd go down a little. The snow packed here and not there. Doin' this I got to Trapper's Creek and it was all flooded cause of McGuiness' dam, so I had about three-quarters of a mile to go across this glare ice to hit the other side of the river where my trail was. It was *where* to hit the trail on the other side. Here was the ordeal. I knew I had a great spruce tree on the lefthand side where I went up the trail and the bank was pretty steep. That trail was about thirty feet up and I had the spruce tree well-blazed, that was my marker.

I had an idea in my memory, just how far to go, how many steps and I put my hand out and I felt the blazes. Well, my god, from there on I relied on my snowshoes tappin' and the dog. After a while, my other dogs, I could hear them barkin' but I still had to go down the rapids there where I had my camp and the water never froze in winter; it was always fast, fast water. Once I hit the water then I got to the dogs with the noise. I was blind then and I walked along 'til I'd found the string I'd run down to the rapids from the cabin to get my water and I followed it up. As luck would have it, I had quite a lot of wood cut.

I was there for about five days, but I couldn't tell darkness from daylight. I nursed myself pretty well, not panickin', and soakin' with them old tea bags. After I had brewed tea I used to put them bags on my eyes at night when I was sleepin'. There was tannic acid in tea and always when we were youngsters, when Grandma was old, with anything in your eyes you put tea bags on them.

Finally one day, I saw it gray and it started to lift again and I could see. What I did right away after my eyes were good I came out of the bush.

When I got back to Cochrane, they'd auctioned everything off. Everything there was. All my machines, stock, furnishings, personal belongings and all they got was $97. The auction man had been selling whole cases of brand new shoes for 10 cents. That's what his bill was and he got enough from the sale for that.


I knew Grey Owl personally. He was an Englishman. I think he's wrote about three or four editions. I knew him ever since he came down to Temagami. I came in 1925. Grey Owl was up at Bear Island. Old Angel died last year. That was the first Indian girl he married. He was a bigamist. He was a remittance man and he came over an accomplished pianist. I know when he got married there it was really a mock marriage. They started to go up on the *Belle*, a steamboat on Lake Temagami. Captain Marsh was the captain on the boat, so there was a great big boozin' party, that's what it were. They all got drinkin' and what not. Belaney was his real name, Archie Belaney. He was in the party so they performed a mock marriage and they went through all the ceremony and they got Captain Marsh to sign so it was legal. That's how Grey Owl came to marry Angel. She was an Indian. So then he went native.

He had a prominent nose like Durante and the Indians were goin' to kill him because he quarrelled with his wife and he started messin' around with other women. He took off and paddled right out of town and went west. That's when he met the other Indian, White Swan. Then he got the job lookin' after the beaver sanctuary. That's how he made his name and he decided to write a book. He started to breed them. He went over to England, you know, when the Indians had the grievance, and he was presented in front of the King and he was like the Indian Chief representing the Ojibway tribe, and they didn't even know he was an Englishman.

I used to be head guide at Camp Whitebear. That was a very exclusive camp, you know, and Benson, the owner, well, they attribute him of being the father of all the symphony orchestras in the States, and that camp was built for the Hollywood clientele.

I've guided quite a few of them, took Nelson Eddy out fishin'. Veronica Lake, Deta Turban. They used to come up and assume names, they didn't want no publicity. The singing barber—that was during the war, Mary Pickford and Douglas Fairbanks. Oh, we used to get quite a few of them. I took them out fishin'. To me they're just ordinary people and I can't see why they're idolized.

I used to take them out fishin' in the evenings. I had some of my dogs take 'em down, sleigh dogs and huntin' dogs, two bucks a day to give atmosphere. It cost about $100 a week. That's away before the war. They had open fireplaces in the cabins, hot and cold water showers. They were really fixed up.

I can remember when the nuclear thing was on and I took out about twenty-five of these guys from where they're making the atom bomb. They used to come up, two or three in each group, but they spoke and they weren't doin' too much fishin' and all they were talkin' about was physics. I used to think they were crazy. I was with them. They'd come up for eight or nine days and they'd all get together and discuss from different laboratories, go into the bush and discuss.

I used to meet quite a lot of prominent people, like a widow woman from the Scarfe paints company, the multi-millionaires. I used to cater to them. They didn't want nothin' to do with the Indians. I had to take them out fishing. We used to have lunch boxes. I can adopt myself to anything, how rough or what. I used to have to pack my own lunch, naturally. I'd swipe a tablecloth and ground sheet and when we came to have shore lunch I'd clean the fish and set a nice table. While the Indians oh! they'd go out and they wouldn't even wash their hands, and they'd eat the fish with pine needles stuck to it.

They used to stay a month or two months, so you got to know a lot of people. Veronica Lake. They gotta talk or remain numb. Even if the fish was not biting, I always make a point of takin' them and showin' them things of interest—like, oh, see that place, there's beaver workin' there, that's an otter slide, and I get 'em interested in botany and explaining the type of flowers, herbs. That's what makes a party, like a guide entertaining people.

Then later on in the evening when they do start to bite, you take them there. There's one guy from the States, a barrister, President of New York Central Railways. He's the one what tried all the German criminals after the war. He's a supreme judge. I was guiding him for over ten years.

Do you want to hear a poem I wrote about the camp?

Tonomo is the place to go
In spite of Abie's verses.
His cabins are cosy,
Your cheeks will be rosy,
And he doesn't rob your purses.

Now when he tells you
The deer abound by hundreds in the fall,
From Wilson Lake and Christie
(And not forgettin' the hole in the wall),
Now don't start lookin' elsewhere
To find some place to go,
But you know what Abie's talk is,
And it's well-named Tonomo.

Now he'll sit and yap
About the mink he trapped
And the wolf and the fox he snared
And the big black bears he follows
'Til he gets them in their lairs.

With his birch-bark horn,
He calls the lordly buck and doe,
But to anyone who really knows him,
It's still pure Tonomo.

Now some are good at shootin' the bull
And they spread it on quite thick;
But Abie's got them all beat
'Cause Abie makes it stick

But just to tourists only,
'Cause they are not in the know,
But to anyone who really knows him,
It's still pure Tonomo.

Beaver castors. The Indians used it a lot for all kinds of medicine, internally and externally. According to the Indians, beaver feed on poplar, and according to the Bible, as I can hear, that's what the cross was made out of: poplar wood. They figure there's a lot of medical properties in it. The castors are the scent glands, the oil gland. They use it like callin' cards. Every other beaver that comes along will call and they'll all get together. The Indians started using it as medicine and it works wonderful. You dry the castors. In the beaver sales they're goin' as high as $30 a pound. They've got good retaining properties. People use 'em to make really high-grade perfume. I've taken it inwardly for backache. I cut a piece and roll it like a pill. Also, I hear it's one cure they figure on for, what you call it, tuberculosis.

There was a time I had another boy with me. We'd stopped trappin' and were in an old lumber camp. Lots of porcupines, they go after old camps, and Charlie, the boy, he was chasin' these here porcupines. I was skinnin' beaver and Charlie climbed up on this old stable and he jumped down, right on an old two-by-four with a great spike, and it went right through his foot out through the laces of his boot.

I laid down and got his foot to me and with my two feet against him and hauled it out. We was spring trappin' and we didn't want to lose any time 'cause you only got about three weeks. I cured it, cut one boot off and used beaver castors. It really works.

I've needed a doctor sometimes, right here. I poisoned myself about five years ago. Ptomaine poisoning. It was wintertime and I opened up a can of tomato juice not knowing it had been frozen and I had a bottle of Worcester sauce and I didn't detect it. So I started out on the skidoo to set these traps and I started to blacken out, got dizzy and the first thing I knew I was vomiting blood and I had to quit the traps. I got the skidoo turned round but I fell off five or six times, blacked right out. Blood out of my face. I had a five-gallon can of coal oil by the stove and I opened the door and I was just to give it a boost with the coal oil and the goldarn can exploded in my hand and I was on fire, and all the beams and my bunks, so I run outside and put myself out. The whole place was on fire. I was half dead.

And I looked, all my possessions is in there, guns, everything. I opened the door wide and I just filled the place with snow, shovellin' and put it all out and collapsed on the bed. I don't know how long I was there, maybe two or three days. An old guy showed up a few days later and he found me. Everything was out and I was stiff. It was about 30 below zero. He got the skidoo and threw me on and took me down to the pipeline and then to the hospital. So I was in there for twelve weeks. I was lucky to pull out of that one.

# Len Doan
## On The Back Porch

The dog and I go to bed together when it gets dark. He folds like a hen. He's quite a pup but he's company. He's got a basket in there he had when he was small and he likes it. Now it's got too small but he still wants to sleep in it. His head hangs out one end and his tail out the other. He can't understand that he grew.

Fat people don't wrinkle. A thin person looks older than they actually are. I'm fat, always was fat.

# Maggie and her Old Man

I'm sitting with Maggie in the kitchen and she's sweating out this morning like a bad fever, her floral dress flimsy with the heat, canopying over a pair of thick legs set a foot apart out of necessity. Too damn hot. No good for talking. Fred, tilted in the armchair, leans on his knees, spitting out the cough that kept him awake most of the night

We're here, the three of us, drinking on a second pot of tea. "Some times, eh, Maggie?" says Fred. He's been telling me how he was orphaned and taken in by a Cree family. How they moved in the night behind the deer, packing all they owned on a pole sled and setting up camp, ten of them all rolled shoulder to foot inside the tepee. This is most of what he can remember, not much more.

Maggie's nodding, stuffing back the photographs in the shoebox, the ones she uses to help her remember. Six children in all and their children, besides. There'd been Sheila and Jimmy up at Moosonee and Barney, her Hollywood boy who went to Florida to sing rock. She's short on explaining because the old man, she says, does most of the talking and he's in the bush cutting wood for their next winter's trapping season. That's up Abitibi Lake where he married her about fifty-five years ago, just after her thirteenth birthday.

Maggie's got it in her head she wants me to meet the old man. Surprise the old man in the bush. So we get moving, the four of us, Fred, Maggie, Shelly, a five-year-old visiting granddaughter and myself. Maggie disappears to the upstairs, reappearing in heavy black pants, side-zipped and safety-pinned, securing the extra pounds for the trip, the pants ending somewhere on the inside of two blue skidoo boots. She's pencilled in her brows and as she goes out the back door, passing close, I think I smell some perfume.

We're hoisting Maggie into the front seat of the truck like a medieval jouster. Driving forty miles east out of Cochrane, leaving asphalt and running on sand and hearing Fred drink down a bottle of wine he bought instead of his medicine. Maggie, up front, sweating and swearing, her hair pushed up under a fisherman's hat, and me thinking, we're heading nowhere, after the last fork in the road where we turned onto grass track. "Over there by those cedars," says Maggie, "that's where I keep my paddles." So everyone's out, Maggie grabbing her canoe supports for the mile-and-a-half hike into camp. Surprise the old man.

Maggie sets the pace because she knows the trail, so we're walking slow enough for the flies to crawl in our hair. Buzzing, circling, enough to make you go mad, bug-crazy, swatting just to keep them from sticking inside the ears. Maggie's rolling from one paddle to the other, Maggie's unbuttoning her blouse, Maggie's sweating breasts through a white brassiere.

Down a foot into muskeg and I've already counted five species of fly. Partridges pumping like old motors off in the bush to my left, and I'm thinking what Maggie said about watching for fresh bear tracks. Something to do with a late spring and the bears being starved for food. "Don't go so fast," Maggie's yelling me back, and I see I've wandered ahead in desperation. Fred collapsing on a tree stump, heaving so bad he can hardly roll his cigarette. Maggie stopping long enough to collect her breath to damn the heat. Never go to the bush this time of year. Shelly whimpering steadily, as she's been doing ever since she went down a rabbit hole an hour back.

Got to see the old man. We all get up at the same time, but it's the walking that strings us out. Once you get the pace going, you have to keep up the swing: squish, squish, rock, squish; and it gets so that you don't want to give it up. Maggie's yelling again, but this time, pointing her paddle to the left, up the hill to the tall pine but no further. I move fast, because the leaves up there show a breeze.

From the top I watch them pulling up behind; Shelly first, Fred next, flat to the hill, and Maggie still breaking brush down in the swamp. We wait for her to take us out to Lake LaFrance.

The old boat's at the clearing and we balance off to keep it afloat, Maggie taking up the middle seat, Fred at the back kicking in the tin motor, byjeezing it and settling for an oar to paddle us up the lake.

The water's still and white with poplar fluff and there's no telling where the trees end and the lake begins. Maggie, whispering about an old Indian gravesite on top of the hill to the right, by the granite rock. The old man will be surprised. Then, round the bend to the left where the jack pine floats out from shore, "There's the old man," says Maggie, and I see him coming down from the cabin, baggy pants flapping at his boots, arms waving out of a torn tartan shirt. Our hellos echoing up and down the lake.

So we're sitting at the table getting drunk on warm beer. Trapped inside this hot little logging hut with its windows shut and sealed with plastic, not daring even to go out for a pee in the dark for fear of being eliminated by mosquitoes. The Coleman light keeps a steady hiss and nobody's much interested in talking but the old man, his face hollowed out by shadows from the lamp, sometimes lost in his own pipe smoke. Maggie's restless, near panic with the heat, and Fred's passed out on the front porch, with only his shoes off, stretched stiff on an air mattress. There's silence from Shelly's room now, ever since we told her we'd feed her to a moose. I'm sitting close enough to the old man to smell a good day's liquor on him and Maggie catches it too. You can tell by the way she's stalked into the bedroom. "Goddamn heat. Got to come here just so's you'll change your underwear. Never again."

And the old man talks on about his Indian mother who told him to stay put in Abitibi. No use going out to civilization when you can make your own life here, trapping and feeding in the wilds. And he talks about Maggie, how she can trim a beaver better than most men can.

"To bed," says the old man, and I say yes and he turns down the lamp, padding into Maggie's room and I watch the millers wing around the ceiling, their shadows bat-size from the blue flame before it goes out, taking us all into the darkness. I've got the couch in this room by the wood stove. It's jammed to the wall in such a way that I've got to sleep with my arms crossed over my chest, almost coffin-like. I'm sure Fred's going to die in the night, choking on the cough he brings up every five minutes. Maggie's snoring and the old man too, and everything in the cabin seems to be drawn up one enormous nose at once, shattering the stillness with a giant snore as it all breaks loose.

It's nine o'clock and the old man's passing round the heel of cherry brandy he forgot to finish last night, timing it with Maggie's departure for the john. We all take a swig and nibble on cold chicken for breakfast. It's been decided we're going up the lake to see the Americans who run Abitibi Lodge. It's three hours by boat and we'll be back at six. It's another plan of Maggie's, who's back filling in her eyebrows again, adding some lipstick this time, warning the old man he better change his clothes and shave. Got to look good for Pete Hughes.

Up-river on five horsepower, past Maggie's trapline, the old man's trapline, the beaver dam where they shot the bull last fall. "There'll be good ones this winter, Maggie. Lots of beaver. And those are Maggie's roses, them wild red things. And the raspberries are coming out too. See where the beavers put the log upstream. We'll have to clear that out. And the moose have been here. See how they've nipped at the water lilies. They like those buds."

The river opens up into Abitibi Lake and to the right, where the reeds are high, is the best spot for shooting duck. Fred knows and the old man agrees; he's been guiding in this water for forty years. Fred hasn't been at it that long, because he took to booze.

There's a rock on the horizon where Maggie says they honeymooned. And a beach beside it where they used to swim. The sun's blazing on the lake and I'm getting a headache from the brandy. I expect to be sick.

I can't remember much of the Americans. I guess it was Pete Hughes who gave us some beer and there was the polaroid picture his sister took from the dock. Five of us in the boat, smiling, a little overexposed, or maybe we were pale anyway. There's not much to tell of the trip back except for Maggie. She was storming. The old man was drunk and Fred wasn't much better. "The old man's not like he used to be," she said. "He changed. Never coming back."

I figured we were moving out of camp before dark and the dark was already moving in. Black clouds smelling of rain. We got Fred into the boat and I oared back to the trail, leaving the old man as we'd found him. Rain peppered the lake, but once you got soaked through, it was warm and kind of comforting. At least it kept the bugs off.

We lost Fred several times on the trail. I looked back once and he was weaving, sideways, but keeping in a straight line. Then, suddenly, he got a spurt going, and he was up with us, slapping me on the back, praising the good Lord, and saying he'd been cured. He pounded his chest and there was no wheeze. He'd been cleaned right through as if by a bolt of lightning. Throwing his stick away, he started running up the path, leaving Maggie and me open-eyed with disbelief. He was back in the truck half an hour before us, and when we climbed in he was still praising the good and great Lord.

We headed back to town and back to Maggie's. I ended up in the nearest provincial park for the night. That's where I am now, soaking, bone-cold, looking at this picture with a flashlight, my teeth clacking like a typewriter, zipped into a sleeping bag and thinking Maggie must have a lifetime of stories. If only she could have remembered them back in the kitchen, I wouldn't be here writing this now.

# Bill Smith
## The Canoe Maker

The thing here is to explain Bill Smith. That first day I walked into the Temagami Boat Works his log cutter had busted and he was sweating over the machine, blowing the pipes clean, rubbing spit on the washers, never quitting until the old diesel engine fired up. The belts started running, clackety-click clackety-click, and the old canoe-maker got up, wiping his hands on his shirttail, impressed with his victory once again over the machine. I figured he'd seen me because he was motioning me to sit on the bench, where he could hear why I'd come. He stood there, magnificently reducing a large plug of chewing tobacco to brown juice, his mouth working like a belly dancer. But it was his look that went square between the eyes, scaring up your insides, that made you keep a distance. Or it could have been the darkness of the place, almost medieval, with small square windows shooting in a yard of light here and there, and the thick low beams bending the length of the ceiling.

He spewed out the juice two feet from my right and asked if I was good luck or bad. I forget my answer but he said I could stay. There was something about the man, the way his short grey hair stood in blades from sweat pushed off his forehead. Those arms tattooed blue with mermaids and the belly that almost hid a half-zipped fly. Something essential, primeval. Why should I know about his life? Is it my business he was born in Great Whale River? He'd question and wait, that was his way. I said nothing, for he somehow knew what I'd say. "All right," he said, "I see what you're thinking." And in this strange manner he worked at keeping me there.

He showed me a new canoe, the white canvas healing on the ribs, and he talked of how his heart and soul went into its making and when it is sold, how a piece of him goes out the door. He showed me how every piece of wood was the very best, no warps, no defects. I had the feeling he was determined to find the same perfection in people and was just as careful about his selection, always choosing and testing the good from the bad, the honest from the dishonest.

His life's work he learned at the age of eleven from his father, a Scot who married and lived with the natives at the mouth of the Great Whale. He knew I could understand, he said, and those eyes burned again in the half-light. He'd gone sour on the Indians. There was too much drink and too much sex, and he warned if I was heading up that way, like Moosonee, I was to stay off the toilet seats. The place was wild with gonorrhea.

I took it as paternal advice, though I wondered about it after. He said he had to collect muskrat from his river traps at noon, so he'd be leaving, but for the rest of the morning he'd talk about communism and his visit to Cuba, his admiration of Castro and his disgust for King Richard.

The next time I saw Bill Smith was in his cabin, and he sanctified the afternoon with a bottle of whiskey, a rare occasion, as he'd been known to reserve it mostly for himself. Perhaps this was the difference on that June day. I only half-remembered the stories from town, that he couldn't separate his reading from his reality. There was a strange vitality about the man. He talked about his mother in the Arctic, how she'd taught him to respect the mind, how they'd understood each other by their silence. He was saying he could describe anything in my mind if I was to concentrate. Well, I thought about a fish fry and before I knew it he was saying he could have cooked those fish better than that. He wanted to teach me how to harness this power, work at it, somewhere in the bush, bed down under the stars. No, I was to get that thought out of my mind because he was too old for it, but it was only out there in the silence of the bush that the mind was free. Sort of an extrasensory perception. That communication had to exist; language was too clumsy for man. We talked that way most of the afternoon, this man and I, the birds pecking at the feeders, the motor boats fantailing up the lake, and the thing here is to explain Bill Smith.

# Dandelion Wine

2 quarts dandelion flowers
(measure without pressing down)
1 gallon of water
Boil for 30 minutes.
Strain out flowers, add
6 cups white sugar and boil ½ hour again.
Let it cool to room temperature
and add 1 package of yeast, the juice
of 3 lemons and 3 oranges.
(Rinds can be added too if desired.)
Let set 9 days and then bottle.

# Lorne Saunders

The man at the Moosonee railroad station said Saunders lived at the end of Reveille Street, on the other side of the gasworks, where the road ran into bush. He assured me the old fellow had some stories, but that it was too bad I'd missed Mrs. Louttit by a week. She was an old-timer too, but they'd buried her last Wednesday.

As I walked towards the bay a couple of Indians raced past me on mini-bikes in a drag match down the main road. There was salt in the air and I could see anchored seaplanes nodding in the grey water. When I turned left, down past the white clapboard church I saw the scarred hulls of fishing boats pulled up on land to die and heard the choking growls of Siberian huskies staked to the ground.

It was there behind the gasworks, a small tar-paper shack painted green with windows trimmed in red. The sidewalk was made of plywood raised a foot above the garden of onions and potatoes. I knocked on the door and from somewhere inside I could hear the squeaking of a rocker and a thin voice telling me to come in. I lifted the handmade latch and stepped into a room five feet square. To the left behind the door was a wall of firewood. To the right was another door bolted with a wooden latch. The old man had written his diary in a heavy right-handed slant into the wood. It was a code of dates and times, with the odd sentence in case he might forget the why of it.

*June 28 1959   there's ice in the rain barrel*

The voice squeaked again to come in. My hand pushed the door open, missing a clutter of moths and butterflies stuck with hatpins above the latch. No one was there, nothing but shelves lining the walls, crammed with a lifetime collection. Four china rabbits sitting inside the ragged jawbone of some prehistoric fish. Trudeau's signature hastily torn from a magazine and taped below a ledge of crusty fossils. There was a chip from a Douglas fir and the flat crossgrain of a tree stump well into its second century. A petrified snail, a dead frog strung by the leg hanging near the window and a clothesline of five dead shrews pegged by their tails.

To my left was a third door leading to the inner sanctum, bolted as the others were with a wooden latch. Inside I could hear the regular squeaking and ticking of something that was very much alive. I flipped the catch. Morning light flashed into the room through the width of the open door, enough that I could see the old man, overgrown by a white beard, rocking incessantly. There was a thick smell of burning wood and a pot of beans sitting halfway down the hole in the stove, black from the fire.

"Are you the undertaker's daughter?" he asked. No I wasn't, he reckoned, for the undertaker who had buried his mother had gone back to Owen Sound. He got up from the rocking chair and closed the door, pointing me to his only other chair. The two small windows crawled with vines and pink flowers, a green-thumb miracle when you considered the surroundings. Two clocks ticked loudly on the wooden table, same time, almost the same ticking.

This third room was wallpapered in magazine cutouts and four calendars, one dated 1957. I asked him about the picture of Bertrand Russell. "Oh, he's dead. I don't know what he done. No idea what he done." There was a rubber spider and a crayfish sealed in a plastic bag nailed to the wall next to a patch of brown fur, stretched and skinned, the size of a child's hand.

"I'll tell you what that is. Four or five years ago we had a plague of lemmings, you know that mouse from the far north. And we had a plague of them last fall. They were by the hundreds all over creation and I caught about ninety-five last fall. I had two mouse traps set, and that lad, he come runnin' along in the dark, down in the ditch, and he got a wollop on the nose that knocked him out."

On the wall above the stove was a rack of railroad hats, one gingham embroidered in pink, red and yellow thread, and the other aluminium cloth. He said he'd made them. Next to his pantry (a shelf of bread and tinned meat) was a dustpan, a rusty oilcan from the gasworks next door, pressed flat, with a hanger for a handle.

He asked me just what I was after. Stories? He told them. It was as if he'd been expecting me. He looked at the tape recorder and recognized it as one of them "talkie things". "Git that thing shut on," he said, his voice cracking like a scratchy 78 rpm record. Sometimes he forgot I was even there, or so I thought 'til he'd say, "Never heard the likes of that did ya?" It wasn't really a question, and besides, he'd answer himself anyway, "Of course ya didn't."

Under his black wool vest he wore a tartan shirt peeling at the elbows, a belt hooked around his waist like a giant watch chain. His matching black pants bagged down to the ankles where two small feet in brown frayed slippers kept the rocker in motion, tapping the plywood floor. He was dressed for visitors, though he didn't believe in visiting. He pulled the peak of the red railroad cap a little tighter over his brow, tugged at the engineer's scarf round his neck, a small gold band glinting on his little finger, and assured me he could remember everything right back.


You can't git nobody to go way back in the 1880s and tell all about that widow woman that lost her boy, fell in the hol' of a boat . . .

My time started in 1887 and there's a lot of people don't remember then. I was born in the township of Tepple and my father and mother lived on a rented farm and the township of Tepple is between Owen Sound and Wiarton, west side of the Georgian Bay.

I was born in November at 1887. It must have been a dry year because the next year the grasshoppers came and they sandpapered the country round there and never left anything green. So my folks had to get off of the farm. They had to sell their horses for three dollars a team to save them from fallin' over at home and they had to walk to Owen Sound. There was no trucks nor transportation in them days. They had to go to Toronto with lots more, I guess, for to go to make glue.

My folks had a couple of cattle and they had a mother pig and some baby pigs and they musta moved in the night because they moved across to a vacant place in the township of Sarawak, a poorer place. The people that had homesteaded it in olden times had two brothers, each took a hundred acres and they cut it across and each brother took a half. The one brother, he stood with it and the other, he moved away to the States and never come back. A very fine, good Christian, honest people.

We moved into that house and my mother said they couldn't sell the baby pigs for 75 cents apiece. Well, they only got a dollar and a half for the horses and you only got 75 cents for a two-foot cord of wood. There was no wages and there was no work and everybody was poor. The poverty was something terrible. There was no money at all. And nobody helped each other because you couldn't help your own self.

I remember my mother. I musta been past eighteen months old when they killed the mother pig. My father got somebody to help him kill the mother pig, that was in the fall. I couldn't talk, but I was out the back door, a little wee kid about as big as a wristwatch and I had dresses on. I wore dresses 'til I was three or four years old, I can remember that. And I was standin' with my back to the north and lookin' westward to where the barn was, and the road was this way, and when the rig went to town, it went past the back door. I remember my mother took me and the baby into the pantry so's we wouldn't hear the pigs squealin'.

Then my folks had meat, you see, and they had lard to fry with whatever they had to fry. They had a bit of garden but I don't know how good or bad it was.

Well, they only stayed there a year or so and then they moved into the that same township again in an old log house. I suppose they paid five dollars a year for rent. But the one day before they had to move over to the log house, the old bachelor, Tom Walker, he came down from up on kind of a hill place, his farm was up on a hill. And then there was a lower farm that belonged to the Gunns—(G-U-double N). He was tellin' my folks (I heard him tell it, but I couldn't say it, but I remembered it 'til I could say it—put it in the bank 'til I could use it:) how he heard awful screamin' and yellin' over at the Gunn's buildin' and he didn't know what happened and he hustled up and done his chores and went down and Mrs. Gunn was out milkin' a cow in the barnyard. And he went near enough to her not to scare the cow, and he called her by name (whatever it was, I forget, maybe Missus).

"Did somebody get hurt here?" he says. "There was such an awful noise."

"Oh," she says, "I had my baby a little while ago here while I was milkin' the cow. I rolled it up in my apron and it's layin' over yonder on the land grower."

And she was goin' on milkin' the cow, that's how hard up and poor the people were. She had no doctor, no thought of a hospital and was about seven miles from the town anyway. And no phone. There were no wires them days. And that's the kind of hard times the people had to come through to tough it. And if you could tough it, you was tough. And if you couldn't tough it, well, you passed away.

Well, I was comin' seven and they shifted me over with my grandfather and grandmother, back in the township of Sarawak again, and I went to school from there. I done chores, gathered apples in the fall for the pigs. They had quite a big orchard, my grandparents had. They were Scotch, and they worked at it too—they didn't waste their money, don't think they did! But no drinkin' and no smokin'. No visitin'. But Sunday was a big part of our life, we went to church every Sunday.

After a while, my folks moved into town and my father died and my mother kept boarders. She got twelve cents a meal for working men in the freight sheds, fourteen cents for their bed, washed all their workin' clothes for nothin' and got $3.50 a week. For twenty-one meals and seven beds.

When I got to be comin' fourteen I hadn't been to school for two years, two summers. I was big enough to hoe. And turnips was ten cents a bushel on the market, which was a wonderful thing. Now you can't get a turnip for ten cents. You can't get much of a turnip less eighty cents. I don't know what the pataties was worth but for a good big dressed turkey you'd get seventy-five cents.

I quit the hoeing and when I was fourteen and a half years old I was sailin' the Great Lakes on a boat. We took a load of iron ore from Michipicoten on Lake Superior to Estabule, Ohio, and we loaded a boatload of coal and took it to the steel mill in the Canadian Sault. Then we took a load of wheat from Fort William down 'round to Midland, and then I didn't like sailin'. I had no use for too much water. I didn't like the grub, it didn't agree with me. So I quit.

I worked at one job and another and I had my seventeenth birthday in a lumber camp at Hope Bay on the Bruce Peninsula. Another lad and me, we were the pair that sawed logs, and we both had our seventeenth birthday in the lumber camp.


The next fall, I was comin' eighteen, a bunch of us young fellows (teenagers, I guess you call us nowadays), we went west on the harvest excursion. We left Owen Sound on the 8th of August 1906 for the harvest fields in the west. There was enough of us to take up a smoker, all but one single seat. There was six of us and there was one double seat in the smoker we used at night to sleep. We went west to twenty miles this side of Moose Jaw and we spread out there and never seen each other again.

I put in the harvest and got $1.75 a day stukin', then I went to the other side of the track, the north side, and got on a thrashin' gang, pitchin' in the field. There was a bunch of New York Americans (two of them there—one of them drove a team for the company and the other one pitched in the field). And they told me I should take a homestead. So I went down and took the train to Regina and I went to the land office in the middle of September and I took up the homestead (I wasn't old enough yet, but for two months later, the middle of November). They were so glad to get rid of that place and get ten dollars cash, I think I could have beat them down a dollar. They'd had that place since the beginning of the world and nobody'd ever took it before.

I went back and finished the harvest and then I went west and I put a shack on my homestead. Then I went back and visited a day or two in Moose Jaw. I went in the Grand Trunk station, no, no, I mean the CPR station, on the 10th of November, 1906. The harvest is all done and I'm waitin' for to grab the CPR eastbound to use the return end of my harvest ticket. The train come and I got on and the conductor said, "Mister, there's a howlin' blizzard behind us but it'll not catch up to us, 'cause we're too far ahead of it." There's a sad story to tell what did happen that very time then. . . .

So I went home to Owen Sound by Winnipeg and Sudbury and Toronto and home to the end of steel in Owen Sound. I worked in a lumber camp near the Hog's Back (that's a tank range now for the government). They put all them people off their old farms. Some of them had been on there for a hundred years, in the name you know.

Soon I got a chance to take a carload of settlers' effects back to the west and I'd get my trip for nothin', which would save $40 or so, which is about what I'd earned in half the winter nearly at the lumber camp.

I went back west to the end of the trip, Belle Plain. The car went to there, just where I wanted to go. I went west again to my homestead after that, in the first part of May.

I had bought a team of oxen. A fellow made me believe I had to have oxen and it was the last thing I needed 'cause I had no machinery or no nothin', and that just took every cent that I had saved up. I had to trade the oxen off. You can't farm with no money, start in at the top with no money.

So I used to walk to town (four or five miles) and work out and I'd be there at seven o'clock in the morning and work 'til noon and go in and have my meal at the restaurant—all you could get to eat for a quarter. Then I'd work 'til six o'clock and when I got home at night I had $1.25. That's the way I put the summer in.

Well, then I got the deed at four years and I got $900 of a loan, a mortgage. I'd bought horses and machinery, a fanning mill, and had it paid for, and one or two other items I had paid for out of my small wages.

It never rained and the mortgage company kicked me off of the place but they let me keep the shack, which was better than nothing. It was inside anyway, out of the weather. And they let me take it and I put sticks under it and drawed it over onto a poorer place that I had across the road allowance. I built a stable over there, in fact, I was buildin' it up anyways, just ties stuck in the ground here and there, wires and slats, and fill the walls in between, tramp it in with horse manure and straw, anything to make it airtight and stop the storm from comin' in on my horses. I had four horses. I had lots of feed for the horses but I hadn't a thing for myself. So, I bought a cow, a fresh calf cow for $35. The little bit of milk helped me. I had a pasture made and I had a cow or two this dry summer and, of course, they made manure through the pasture.

In the fall, I knew that I couldn't winter above ground. I was twenty-five miles from the nearest tree, there was no wood or no coal, there was no deer and no moose and the rabbits had cancer blisters in the meat, but you couldn't see them unless you cut the meat open and cut into the blister. You could cut a half-inch from that blister and cook that rabbit and eat blister and all, if you didn't know you was eatin' it. So the rabbits wasn't fit to eat. I had $7.13 and I took the team into town and the wagon (I had a democrat and I had it paid for) and I said to the lumber man, Lou Martin, "Lou," I says, "I want you to gather all the broken, twisted, split wood, anything you can't sell to nobody, and I'll take it."

I went back the next day and I says, "Lou, how much will the lumber cost?" He said two dollars. And I had over a thousand feet and some of them was two by eight, two by fourteen, split boards and all manner of the very best of stuff, but it was crossgrained and in the sun it would roll up. One man could stand on the one end of the plank and one on the other and she'd split like a quarter's worth of cheese, cornerways. Well, that you can't sell. I cut off a lot of them sharp points and had them for wood. Then I went home and I dug into the side of a hill and built a sort of alleyway, twelve feet by four feet wide and six feet high and I cribbed that all up good and throwed dirt back in around it again. (But I walked in off the level. I didn't have to walk up to it, I walked in right off the level.) It was twelve feet and there was sort of a projection out of the front, leanin'.

Anyway, I got up on top of the hill and I dug eight feet square back of that and down past the end of the tunnel and I cribbed that all up good and solid and I put the dirt all back in again and I put stovepipes in. Then, at the first of November when the weather got bitter cold, I took my stove, a small cookstove (it was rolled steel), and put it down in there and I made a bed and I was twelve and eight—that's twenty feet underground, and from four to six feet of dirt on top of me. And the cold never got down through. The ground was dry as shovellin' wheat.

So I had 25 acres of wheat in on this poor place and I cut that and I got it thrashed. And I had 73 bushels off of 25 acres, the first crop— there shoulda been far more than that—sometimes I got far more off of two acres than what I got off those 25 acres. Well, I never sold it 'cause it wasn't first class grain and I wouldn't get little or nothin' for it.

I had the granary and a good roof on it, so I put it in the granary. I had a fanning mill shed by its own self, right by the end of the little granary. Good tight doors so no snow blowed in. I had a tettle and I made a little hand sleigh. I took one or two comfort soapboxes (they was made of wood them days, they're not now. No boxes is made of wood nowadays, they're carton boxes) and I went through the pasture and I gathered what they call buffalo chips, that's the Sunday name for it. In a weekday, you can call it somethin' else—cow manure. Some of them was like great big bannocks and some was like layer cakes, you know. And as dry as ever they could be, because it never rained and it never rained all fall and I gathered up a lot of that. That's all I had to burn for the winter. The fire was red hot in under that one lid away back underground.

I rolled my feet in bran sacks and I went to town that way and I lived on boiled wheat and I had $7.13 when the snow come on and when the snow went away I still had four dollars and some odd cents. And it cost me three dollars for winter and I'd built a residence for two dollars and wintered for clothing and food for less than four dollars. Now, you can't do that nowadays. Ate boiled wheat all the time and I never had a cold and never was sick a day. Never went no place because the other people was worse off than you was. There was no old age pension in them days and there was no such thing as relief and soup kitchen and help—that wasn't in the dictionary, because there was no need of it.

So when spring come, I had enough money left to board me while I put my crop in and done a bit of work around and I got two days' job with a man and team on the township road. I earned five dollars for two days.

Well, the other people had a worse time than I had. Eighteen miles east of me they had a big dry spell of a few thousand acres where it never rained. If a cloud would go over and leak a bit, you'd get some good out of it. But there was clouds went over where I was and thunder and lightnin' and a bit of wind and just a few drops. It wouldn't wet your shirt! Well, that don't wet the ground and when you're farmin' you gotta have wet. You gotta have water on the ground. So all of my neighbors east of me was from New York state, they lost their land, one or two farms apiece, just as I did. Everyone of them is dead now, because they were middle-aged people and we were all poor. That's why we went there, to start with 160 acres of land for ten dollars. You can't do that anyplace else.

Then in 1912 when it never rained, eighteen miles east of me one man shot his wife and his five kids and himself. And another one, he shot himself. The old magistrate in my town, Morris, he called the government and he said, "Look, you people had better start and smarten up, the poverty here is terrible. They're shootin' their families and they're shootin' theirselves." So they did.

You signed papers that this mortgage comes ahead of all taxes, all debts and everything else, and I agreed to pay 5% interest. That's government handout in them days. You had to pay that money back at 5% interest. There was no such thing as givin' it away. And I got twelve dollars' worth and wintered on that.

So one man north of me, he had a family and his old father to look after, and he toughed it through the winter, I don't know how. The butcher would give them soupbones and they didn't sandpaper the soupbones them days like they do now, to get the last bit of meat off. There'd be quite a little bit of whittlin's on there and they would get carrots and potatoes and boil up a bunch of soup and have that. I don't know how they wintered.

The next year nobody had shut down on him like they did me. Well, he farmed and he got quite a bit of crop and he drew it to the town and he sold it and nobody watched him and he got the grain tickets, probably a couple of hundred dollars' worth. So one day, he got the grain cheques cashed and he loaded their stuff in the wagon and took one team with the wagon and the family and the old father

63

and went to our town (that's Morris). He put the goods off at the station and the family disappeared at the station while he took the team and put them in the feedbarn. He went over, never bought tickets or nothing. They expressed the stuff to Swift Current and they all got on the train and away they went, grain money and all. So then the mortgage companies and the bank, whatever there was for taxes, soon jumped on everything that was left and it got all divided up.

Now the place was witched and we got two more dry years and I got nothing and I give a quit claim deed of a farm I'd just bought. I'd paid for it all 'cept for $700 and I could have saved it but I could see nothin' to stay in that country for at that time. If you lost one year you went so far behind on everything that if you got one good year that just brought you up even. And nothin' left over. I sold my place, this poorer place I was livin' on, for less than the buildin's cost and I pulled stakes and went back to old Ontario.


In the west (after they put me off that farm over on to the poorer place) we got a craze that they should have the telephone in. They wanted everyone to put one in and some peoples was well enough off, you know, but I was just scrapin' the bottom of the barrel. Lots more was poor too.

So, I got the telephone in and I lived pretty well near the middle of my quarter section. I got the phone in and then I had hard times. Cattle, you couldn't get nothin' for cattle. I come home one night and my telephone was dead. I went over to a friend's and they said they seen them cuttin' my telephone line. They disconnected me off the line. I was about four posts in. I'd pay a dollar or two dollars or whatever I could get, and I had it down to $2.20, my telephone bill, and they come and disconnected me up the road.

Fifty-seven years after that, I was sittin' here the other night, thinkin' what a sleepyhead I was them days.

I got the $2.20 (I think I had to send to my mother to get it in Owen Sound). I think *now* that I should have took the money and went to the post office and got a postal note so's that they couldn't make no mistake. That was the bill. I had it all paid but that. Then I got to pay five dollars to get them to put the wires back on again, you see. And what I should have done, I figured the other night, was to have told them, to thank them for their service, here's your $2.20 that I owe ya and now you have showed me that you can do without me, now to show you that I can do without you—this is a thirty-day notice for to get all the stuff that belongs to the telephone company off of the

northwest quarter 251783 (that's the number of my land). I'll give you thirty days to get everything off of my place. And make them take the whole outfit off of the place and tell them if I miss your companionship too much, I'd go to the schoolhouse and get three or four headlights off of some kid to make up for it and thank you for all your stuff, yours truly.

Now would that ever have been some letter! Well, I thought of it 57 years too late.

I was married in the meantime. We bought a poor place down home in Tepple township. We needed a home and then she died. There was a boy and a girl and my mother looked after them. I come in the north. It was more for keepin' a few head of somethin', a few head of sheep, more than it was for growin', just for hay and stuff.

I was on the farm in Owen Sound in the Hungry Thirties. And that was Indian summer for me. I'd had the flu in 1918 and I never got over it 'til I went back in the fall of '28. I bought a pair of goats and one was milkin', and I started drinkin' goats' milk. Got half a dozen sheep and I bought the hens with the place. About seventy-five hens. Lots of eggs and lots of goats' milk, and I got over my flu (for ten years I had it). I made my own little sawmill so's I could cut my own lumber. I made my own porridge meal. There's no use of me bein' Scotch if I ain't tight enough to use it.

I knew what to do with old horses that should go to the fox farm for heaves. A horse isn't worth nothin' to a farmer if it's heavie. A heavie horse can get the wind in but the devil himself can't get it out again. I knew to feed a horse powdered labillia and a little bit of black antimony in with his chop and that took the heavies all away. I would buy a horse that shoulda went to the fox farm and take him home and cure him and he'd get fat and done all my little bit of work that I had. Put my hay in and took my crop off and done my ploughin' with these old horses that shoulda been eat by foxes.

So I put in the Hungry Thirties. I sold the place and I come north. I was a provincial police guard for a while at the Abitibi Canyon and I didn't care much for that. Then I got on the government fire towers and I put in 16 more years on fire towers lookin' for smoke.

You never shook hands with a ghost nor a witch nor ever had one take a hold of you? Aha, well, I may be the only person on this street that had a hold of a ghost and the ghost had a hold of me. That was the year I was on Ghost Mountain. That's a witchy pace that's on the far side of Lake Abitibi.

I didn't get my old tower that year—they put me on Ghost. It's 1,820 feet to the top of the rock and it's eighty feet to the tower, that's 1,900 feet. Anyway, Indians won't stay there 'cause it's witchy. So I never was ascared of the ghost and I was in bed and I had a good sleep and I lay on my right side to sleep and then I woke up somewheres around midnight and I laid on my back awhile and rested and then I laid on my left side and rested, and then I turned on my back and rested again, with my hands folded always like that on my chest and my eyes shut. (I never keep my eyes open at night, maybe open them, but I shut them again.) And the blankets was up over my hands and I was layin' there with my eyes shut and these two cold hands come along and took hold of me like that, round my neck. I just reached up and grabbed a wrist in each hand in the right place and I yanked and they were as cold as dead meat. And they were a woman's wrist. Let me feel yours. That's exactly that size. Maybe it was you.

Well, anyway, the wrist was gone. You can't hang onto a ghost 'cause he ain't nothin' in the first place. And they were gone out of my hand just like nobody's business and the hands was gone off my throat too. But I wasn't disappointed that they went either. I'm not no braver than nobody else. But I wanted to hang onto that bloomin' thing and talk to it and see what made it want to live a life like that. But I wasn't snoopy enough to get up and walk around the house and see where the blazes she went to. I wasn't snoopy enough for that! I stuck with the bed. That was the last I ever heard of the ghost.

And a week after that I was layin' in the same position again, with my eyes shut. I'd been asleep and rolled over on my back and I musta been awake, when the blankets started to go and I grabbed a handful of the blanket cloth and yanked it back up to its place again. I wasn't nosy enough to get up and go around and see what was at the foot of the bed, don't think I was! But I wanted to talk to that ghost in the worst way and I would like to have tied it up and tamed it, just for fun.

The Indians won't stay in there. The year before I went in, there was five on that tower but they'd never said if they'd got caught by the witch, they never let on.

There was supposed to have been a woman murdered in there in olden times, about the time the white people come to this country, maybe 150 or 200 years ago. Supposed to been, the story was. But you can't hear that from everybody.

I was right in the middle of the Abitibi. There's twenty million, seven hundred thousand acres of bush. I had lots of company, moose and bears, and I never made a noise and there was chipmunks down at the cabin. And one chipmunk, I'd call him, "Kitty, kitty, kitty," and I'd throw a piece of bread and when he heard the kitty, kitty, kitty, and seen the bread, he'd go and look and I got him so's he'd knowed his name was Kitty.

I never fooled him. And I had been away for a year and come back on the tower again. He was over on a stump, chomp, chomp, and I went out the door, "Kitty, kitty, kitty," and he says, "Oh, boy, the same voice," and I'd throw the bread. As soon as it would land near him, he was comin' and he'd grab it and head for the bush. He was a friend all summer.

And them partridges used to hatch within twenty feet of the back door. And there was partridges and rabbits and I never made a noise. And the confounded bear, he would come too, and I didn't want *him*.

One day I was walkin' up to the tower and I had a staff stick. That's not a walkin' stick, that's a staff stick, straight with one limb cut off two inches long, so your hand won't slip down and you can slope it anyway and it's half a horsepower help to get along. And walkin' along, not makin' a speck of noise, and here's a bear come walkin' out near as half as high as I was. And I hauled off and hit the top of the staff on his head and did he ever get in the bush and woof and jump and run. He quit the woofin' and I thought maybe he'll come back. And I stood there and in a minute he come walkin' out on a high bluff of rock right in front of my face. He was mad at himself to think that he was foolish enough to run and he didn't know what from. Well, I thought this was it. And I never said a word. I was never so scared in my life. I knew that I'm a goner and I set some stuff down and I was half a mile from my own shanty. I had a rifle in there.

He started to come down off of the rock and I made up my mind quick, I'm goin' home. And I couldn't run much 'cause I had to keep one eye ahead to watch where I'm goin', and one eye behind to watch where he's comin'. I didn't want to get a grab in the hind end and not be lookin'. He never followed close enough, but when I went back up with the rifle, there's his bear footprints on my path in the dust. He went on up into the bush and I never seen him again.

A beaver family moved into the little lake right back of the tower down about 1,000 feet and they dammed the creek goin' out of it and then the lily pads started to grow that summer and the moose started to move in there because they could stay in the water and eat lily pads.

You see, the bulldogs gets in between their hind legs and when there's bare meat, they'll bite. That's horseflies, bulldog is what we call it. But they're real horseflies and they're terrible. They come here just about two days ago.

There was two mother moose had two babies each, that's four. There was three mother moose had one baby each, that's three. Pretty soon, the mother moose would leave her little baby and she would go and have a feed and she'd hustle home. Home I call it to where the baby was. Well, then I could tell the baby's gone, 'cause she never went home. She would eat and go someplace else. The baby's ate. And then maybe one of the mothers that had two (one baby, he's gone), she brings the other baby with her then. After a while, they're all gone, but maybe one or two mothers has each one left and after a while, the seven baby mooses is all gone. And all the time I was there, I never knew of only one mother to raise her baby to put on his winter coat. The bears eat them.

I liked that tower life. I could see way over into Quebec and they settled Quebec away southwest of Noranda, a wonderful chunk of clay land. And I could see the smokestack at Noranda and I could see the smokestack at the Beatty mine and part of a buildin'. Miles and miles away. Oh, I liked that life.

One day, I thought there's two bears down in the lake fightin'. Here it wasn't bears at all, it was two otters havin' roughhouse. (I thought I never seen bears crazy enough to go out in the water and start to fight, 'cause it's not their kind of business.) No, there was five of them altogether, five otters. I seen one of them and he had something white in his mouth and I could see he got a sucker for to eat.

That's how I've been foolin' in my life.


I come sixteen times to Moosonee, and I went out fifteen. Now if I didn't have the north in my blood, I was workin' it up, wasn't I? I musta been, 'cause I never went out the sixteenth time.

And I like it here. I got a letter from a woman down home a year ago and she said, "Lorne, you wouldn't like it here now." She says there's some of them that's barefooted and long hair and dirty clothes. She says a terrible-lookin' sight of people. I guess they're hippies, whatever that is. It's some kind of a thing that fell off of a star and took light somehow.

When I come here there was no settlement, just a settlement of tents. Well, the TNO got at you (know the TNO? Temiskaming and

Northern Ontario, now it's Northland but I still say TNO). The TNO took and surveyed the town lots on the far side of the creek, from the railroad down to the big river. They put the Indians across there on their own lots. You can go from the end of the town here for 4,000 miles into Alaska and you don't need to put a foot on nobody's place that pays taxes. And you can go from here to the DEW line, up near Russia (wherever that is), on the ice and there's no settlements of any kind.

Two years ago or a little more, I was walkin' on wet sand and I stepped the next step with my right foot and there was water in the sand right to the top and I didn't know it. My foot went down about two inches more than it shoulda went and it pulled my leg out round the hind-end joint (or whatever you call it) and I couldn't walk with it that way and I stood on her, trapped her back into place and there's the way she's pointin' now. I can't go stealin' at night anymore, they'll know my tracks.

Then my left hip shoulda been broke four times. It wasn't broke at all but I guess it was bent a little bit and the arthritis got into it somethin' terrible. And it got into the marra in the middle of that bone. (The marra in the back of your spine, that's fer sendin' the message, if you get your foot hurt, the message will come up through there and into your head.) Arthritis will get into wherever you got a hurt.

And tryin' to sleep at night and everytime the heart would beat there was a telegram that would go down the marra right to the foot. Unmerciful, just like turnin' a wire around a little wee bit.

When I went back to Owen Sound on one of my trips out, there was a fat old German on the street. He knew me and he knew that I was away in the wilds and that I would have somethin' to tell him. So he wanted to talk to me. He says, "I had a hard time this year." He's a fat old fella, too heavy, and he said, "They put me in the hospital for three months for arthritis and then they told me to go on home. They can't do nothin' for you."

So he went home with his arthritis and he met another old fella who says to him, "Why don't you get a bit of oil of eucalyptus and take about ten drops at night for three nights and miss three nights, add a little sugar before you go to bed." And the German fella says, "I did and I'm dandy now."

So I went to the drugstore in Owen Sound and I said, "Mister, do you know some kind of medicine called, ah, encylapedia or somethin'?" He says, "Oil of eucalyptus." "That's it," I says. "Now is that poison?" He says, "Not if you don't take too much of it." It's from the eucalyptus tree in Australia and I think maybe they have some in California. The eucalyptus tree is a big green tree with a big heavy leaf on it. I said, "That fat old German cured his arthritis with that. Takes ten drops at night on a bit of sugar. Would you sell me some?" He says, "A little bottle will cost you a quarter."

So I took it and I came back north and built a cabin up here at Otter Rapids. I was takin' oil of eucalyptus and I thought one night there's no pain in my leg. I'd forgotten about it. Then I met an old Frenchman and he had arthritis and I said I'd go to the drug store and get some oil of eucalyptus. And I told the coroner (he was the doctor), "Have you got any oil of eucalyptus?" He says, "Yes." I says, "The fellow over here's got arthritis. I cured myself with that, took ten drops at night on a bit of sugar." The doctor says, "If you wasn't half moose, that would've poisoned you." Well, I said, "It didn't kill me but it moved the arthritis out."


I think I'll tell you a story. Last fall in the warm weather when the three wooden doors was all open and the screen door was shut (it shuts its own self), there was a rap on the door and I went and shoved it open. Two men standin' there. I says, "Come in." I give one the rocking chair over yonder and the other one this bench over near the stove and they never said nothin'.

I knew what they were after. They had been askin' themselves, that old man must have some money: he don't play bingo, he don't booze, he don't play pool. They beat an old woman up in Moose Factory for her old age pension and put her in the hospital badly cut up, but she had brains enough to leave the money with someone else.

So, they were lookin' at me, never spoke, and I knew what they were doin' and I'd reach over and get this stick and rap rap on the desk and look right at 'em. Don't think I'm too religious to use it. They knowed it. They stayed for about 50 minutes and after that they got up and went out.

Now I'd like to have one come back and let him sit there for a while and I would tell him, "Look you child of one parent (you know what that is, a child of one parent? Well, he's a bastard.), if you're comin' here to beat me up and get my money you're makin' a big mistake 'cause you're goin' to end up with a lot of broken bones and in the hospital and if you don't believe it, just try it. I'll put you in the hospital and if you can take the money from me, I'll halve up with you, whatever you can get."

I'm waitin' on him now.


Well, I'm goin' to tell you another story, about an Englishman. He was monkeyfiddlin' around 'til he got way down the Mackenzie River to Aklavik. There was a family of Eskimos come in from Victoria Island (about 48 million acres in that island out in the Arctic Ocean or Beaufort Sea or whatever bunch of cold water that is out from our north coast) and they come in and they sold furs to the Hudson Bay trader there at Aklavik. And they were laughin' and carryin' on and not a worry in the whole outfit. They had the north in their blood and he had the north in his blood. He caught on to that too, you see. And he got in with them Eskimos and they adopted him and he went out with the Eskimos and he eat whatever they eat, he done whatever they done, wore whatever they wore. And he's not goin' nowhere and there's nobody comin', that's a cinch!

So after some time he saved up some furs and he went out and took a trip back home to see the folks in the old country. I guess he took some pictures of their buildin's, which would be whaleskin and sealskin and stuff stuck up around some sticks and one thing and another. They'd be some lookin' residences way out a thousand miles from trees!

Well, anyway, he was back to see them and one day he says, "Well, I must be goin'." They say, "You're not goin' back there?" He says, "That's my people and that's my life." He says, "I'm goin' back."


I was here in Moosonee all '56. I put in '57, '58 and '59 on the government fire tower and I was 72 when I quit the fire tower. They don't let nobody on a tower now at 72. So then I come back in the fall of '59. I had a cold in the middle of April when I went out, caught it by goin' on the train and mixin' with people. Here I don't mix with people and now I'm two months and a half in my fifteenth year on two small little colds. What's the secret? Keep away from people. Ya get where there's a gang and somebody's got a bad cold and he'll cough and sneeze and you're sprayed like as if they were sprayin' potatoes fer to poison the potatoes. You're in it and you got it.


This Eskimo from Akapatok Island wanted to go to Pond Inlet, which is on the far northeast corner of Baffin Island which has 129 million acres in it, I think. And there was a store and a tradin' post at Pond Inlet. An inlet is where it's washed out and the tide comes way in there but it's pretty well sheltered from heavy storms. So, they had to go while the ice was on to get across Fox Channel to the mainland on Baffin Island. And they were all in great happiness and they done a lot of sewin' and made goods to go with and they took caribou skins and they soaked them in water down through holes in the ice and got them all soakin' wet, brought them up and they were rolled up and then bent. They bent the one end up and put a weight on it and that made a runner out of this frozen, rolled-up caribou hide.

Then they took two of them. They had lots of lace leather, you see, and when they catch a seal, they'll peel them like you peel an apple and you get fifty foot of lace leather, if you want it. So they used salmon for crossbars on them skins. Of course, the snow was hard and driven hard with blowin' and they loaded up, men, women and kids, and everybody was happy and away they went.

Well, the people at Pond Inlet ain't lookin' for them. And the people here ain't lookin' for them to come back because they're goin' while there's freeze-up and sleighin'. And they had a band of dogs with them too, you see, to draw their frozen seals and frozen fish to eat. They musta had some kind of guns, the oldtime muzzle loaders, musta been.

They were goin' to trade their furs at Pond Inlet and then come back and camp and stay all summer in the middle of Baffin Island and kill caribou and skin and dry them to get hundreds of pounds of meat to bring home when the winter come on the next winter. Nobody here was lookin' for them to come back because they're not comin' for another year yet.

And there was an old man and his wife by the name of Patlock, P-a-t-l-o-c-k or P-a-t-l-o-k. Patlock and his wife was goin' across Baffin Island in the winter too. And their dogs turned and headed fer upwind (that is, goin' against the wind). They thought, well, we'll let the dogs go, there's caribou. Then they seen them ice houses, you know, igloos (I call them ice houses), and they got to them and that's where the smell was comin' from. Dead bones and dead skins and all manner of stuff. And here, in the night, they looked in one of the ice houses. They

says, "Oh, there's somethin' over yonder. A woman alive yet and there's a girl in there and she's alive yet."

So, they're both dyin' of starvation and they asked her what she was doin' there. "Oh," she said, "we piled a cache." You know what a cache is? Blocks of ice and blocks of snow, piled up, and then you put in these skins, hand sleighs and fish for crossbars—you never hear tell of the likes—that's all dog feed! She says they were in their ice houses for the night and the dogs was runnin' loose. Of course, can't tie them up when the ground's frozen—there's no sticks or no nothin'. Everything is eat raw.

She says that one Eskimo, he woke up and there's water drippin' on his face, so he got them stirrin' around and it was warm and they went out and the warm wind from the south had thawed one side of the cache, and the heavy weight up on there squeezed it and down the whole works come and the dogs had eat harness, sleighs, the whole works, and seals and fish. It was all destroyed.

Well, they can't go no place. They have no sleighs. They have no dogs for harness. The harness is gone. They have no feed. They had to stay there and she said, "We eat the dogs first." And then she said, "If somebody is gettin' pretty weak, just as quick as he dies we get at and take the meat off him and eat it." And they had nothin' to cook with. They had to eat that raw meat. Now, that wouldn't be no treat for me or you. Raw human meat—I wouldn't give you five cents a bushel for it!

Well, the Patlocks, they give the girl food, she's dyin' with hunger too, and the stomach—it seems when you start to starve to death and no more come in, your stomach, he quits and he goes all in little. And the girl, they give her a bunch of raw meat, or whatever they had to eat, and she eat quite a bellyfull of it and it killed her dead as a doornail. The woman she knowed better than that, she only eat just a little mouthful and a little bit and she lived. And she said she helped eat her husband and two of her boys. Now, that's not funny.

After she got strong enough, they took her and they went away to . . . (what do you call that town on the east side of Baffin Island, the settlement there? Ah, that's Frobisher Bay. Yah.) And they went away to Frobisher Bay. And they kept goin' and that woman went with them, and them people back there never knew where they ever went to and the people had the store at Pond Inlet never knew where they ever went to and here they were all dead and eaten but one woman and she had got married again.

Now, that's the last of the story and I'm the last one that knows about that story that I know of. You never heard it before. Well, if you live a hundred years, you wouldn't hear it again.


I bought red, white and blue rubber roofin' for my shanty. You never knew you could buy white rubber roofin'? Nobody else did either. I ordered it from Eaton's. And flyin' in an airplane and lookin' down, it must look funny to see red, white and blue.

I find my wood for burnin'. I go out in the winter, go to town, keep my walk cleaned off, maybe five or seven times a day. I don't allow no snow at all on it.

This is the hat I should be wearin' today. You seen it before? I made it. I embroidered it, made the peak. Isn't a wrinkle in it. Made that other hat out of aluminium-painted cloth. Looks like galvanized iron. I gave the pattern to some women and they wanted me to tear one of my hats apart to see how it's made and I said, "To the diggin's with ya." It's supposed to be made like a railroad man's cap. Just puckered in there.

Where did you get that cap? I didn't get it, I made it. Where do you get the water here? I don't get it. The Great Manitou puts it on the roof and I catch it in the rain barrel.

I keep that outside door shut and people don't come at all. I don't want nobody at all.


This here, you know, this is a sea bottom. One day the water was eighty feet deep. That's why you dig down in this stuff, you dig down twelve feet on the bank of the river and if you watch close, you can find a little wee clamshell like your little fingernail. Well, they belonged on the sea bottom of another age.

And when I come by airplane from Fort Albany and the sun was in the westward, you could see puddle holes, you'd think clean to Manitoba, where the water's never got away. You dasn't walk on it, nor a duck don't go on it. It's pure soft muck. And here it's from the ice ages meltin' in Lake Abitibi and all that stuff washed down here and the dirt settled . . . and the far end's the ships' end where the water from there is clean on out. The settlings. There's a name for that. What do you call that dirty water? Sediment. Yes. Well, this is only sediment. For 2,000 years the water's been gone from there. This isn't sea bottom that we're workin' for a garden, that black dirt. That's leaf mould and new vegetation that has grown on top and died down. There's old stumps in here. If you go along that other road back of the shack, you'll see old stumps down three feet. So, in this dirt they growed 'til they suffocated and couldn't grow no longer and then they had to die. Then other stuff growed up and their needles and leaves fell and moss grew and died and more growed on top of it and that died, and more growed on top. It takes about a 100 years for an inch. So, there's about 2,000 years of black muck. You can't grow nothin' in that 'cause it's still full of salt.

Fort Albany up here was built first low down to be near the James Bay. Well, if the tide went out and left his ice in there, then the river broke up, which drains to fifty miles north of Lake Superior. That's a whole continent flooded from here to fifty miles north of Lake Superior and that's God's lake country.

The time I was at Fort Albany, I had dinner at the Hudson Bay Factory's house and a woman (a lovely woman) she told me 'bout gettin' breakfast one mornin', she says, last spring, with the long rubber boots on and the water soppin' under the cookstove, the country was a lake. The tide went out and left the ice across the Albany River and the Albany River makes up his mind he's openin' that day and come down with a mad rush with millions of tons of ice and millions of horsepower and just plugged and flooded the whole works. And it broke their fence down.


One day I had to cut my own hair. I cut my own hair when I was 365 miles from a barbershop. I got kinda hung up in it and an old Russian took pity on me and he helped me. Well, I thought, if I can cut my own hair 365 miles from a barbershop, I can cut it right on the same street as the barber is, and that's what I've done ever since. Since July, 1928. I cut it as long as there's hair and that's as good as anybody can do.


I built my cabin over in the bush and the mad rush came and the Bell Telephone moved into Moosonee. They were puttin' radar stations in the north. Everything was military secret. You mustn't talk about nothin' to nobody. That was about 1955, somewheres about that.

Comin' down on the train, there was a fella with short whiskers and I knew he didn't belong outside. I said, "How far are you goin', Mister?" (On the train, you know, comin' to the north, you can ask anybody where he's goin' and he don't tell you it's none of your business. Like you don't ask him in Toronto where he's goin', he'll soon tell you it's none of your business where he's goin'.) "Well," he says, "I'm goin' to Moosonee." But he says, "I goin' farther."

I says, "You're goin' to that big power plant, that big radar station they're buildin' at Fort Severn."

"No," he says, "I'm not goin' there."

Well, I says, "You're goin' to Great Whale."

"No," he says, "I'm goin' to Winisk." He says he's an engineer but he's got signed papers sayin' that he mustn't speak nothin' about it. He says he ain't supposed to know where he's goin'.

Well, I says, "There's seven fellas goin' same place you are in the next coach here. They're goin' to Winisk, too." And I says, "Earn all you can because they're sendin' $150 million back in there."

When he came to Moosonee, he went into the Bell Telephone (they had a monstrous dose of buildin's here) and he says, "There's an old fella with whiskers come in on the train and he says he can tell me where I'm workin' and how much money we're spendin' and he says I've signed papers that I don't know nothin' about it. He says I mustn't speak and here he knows all about it and he don't belong here at all."

So, a Scotch man from Glengarry, he told me all about it the next mornin'. He says he laughed when the engineer come into the head office of the Bell Telephone and he says an old fella come in on the train and he knows all that's goin' on. Well, I says, "Outside all you gotta do is listen to the radio and the Reader's Digest. If they know anything, they'll tell it. If they know anything, they'll put it in the papers."


So my shack was over there and they were goin' to bulldoze it into the river. They took the bulldozer and put my wood in a gully and covered it all up (my next winter's wood, covered it all up nice—it's in there yet). They were goin' to bulldoze the shack into the river.

The Ukrainian over at the sawmill, he says, "You can't bulldoze a man's shack in the river, you'll get into trouble." The man from the Bell says, "That old man, he don't own this ground and he ain't payin' taxes." The Ukrainian says, "But, look, you don't own the ground and you ain't payin' no taxes."

Well, I had to move my shanty. They put it on skids, brought skids to put under it and drew it way up yonder and I said I'm goin' to try and see if George Stockton will let me put my shack near his place. But then he's got to get out of there too! Well, I says, "I'm not buyin' a town lot. When I get old I'm not payin' taxes. I know where there's millions of acres of country and there ain't nobody on it." Well, the Bell man says, "We'll put your shack up by that coal office."

I said to bulldoze it into the river. The frogs left there three years ago, there was no place for them to sit and croak. No water. Well, he says, "Look, we'll put your shack wherever you want. You get a place and we'll put it there." I said, "Thank you, friend, that's the best you can do."

So I said to Mike the Ukrainian that is dead now, "I'm goin' to see the Father at the mission and see if they'll let me put my shanty on the corner of their warehouse property." When I saw the Father, I said, "I'm wonderin' if you'd let me put my shanty on the corner of your warehouse property over there?"

"Oh, Lorne," he says, "I can't give you permission for that. I got to get permission from higher up." He says, "I'll phone the Bishop in Montreal."

I says, "Forget it. I'll stick a match in it and take the train in the mornin' and beat it. And stay outta here."

"No, no," he says, "don't do that. The Bishop says to tell Lorne he can put his shanty wherever he likes."

So here I am, Presbyterian by birth and livin' on Catholic Church property and I pay no taxes and no rent yet and have my own garden and I'm quite independent. And peoples say, "Where do you get your water?" I says the Great Manitou puts it on the roof and I catch it in a nice, clean rain barrel. And I melt snow in the winter and get wood wherever it is. I said there's millions of wood all over the country fer just goin' and carryin' it home. Yah.

I don't want no supplement—if that means more money. So they give me some, they give me a raise in pension. I wrote them, please don't send any more money. I don't want it. I'm gettin' all I need.

I have no hydro. I come here to get away from white man's inventions. I got no hydro. My mother lived to be 92. She never had an electric washing machine, never had no refrigerator. I have no refrigerator, I have no TV. If they were two for a nickel I wouldn't take one, I have no earthly use for it. I looked at TV one of them three winters that I was in Kirkland Lake on Sunday afternoon awhile and it took me to Monday to get my eyesight back ag'in. But it's a wonderful thing to see a cowboy shoot fifteen or twenty shots out of a six-shooter that's only got six loaded bullets in it. That's a wonderful thing, mind you. You can see that on TV. They'll bang away all fall and never stop to load.

And I never shot a pool ball but there's people I'd pay $25 apiece to shoot and I think that I could settle quite a few labour strikes, get the strikes settled a little quicker by shootin' the right party.

And I was never drunk in my life. No earthly use for drink. I don't want it, if it were even given away free.

And I don't want a car if they were fifty cents apiece. Them swell big cars. I never run an automobile in my life, but I can run the Ford car. You run it with your feet. You put the lever ahead and you run it with your feet, go ahead on low, and let it off with your finger, not with your foot. I bought a brand new Ford one time in the west for $550, firsthand. A Model T double-seater (that's all there were). And I sold it on my way east, the time we left the west.

I don't want a car, not these cars you run with a lever. There's a kind of spirit in them that does all the changin' gears. I don't have nothin' to do with them at all.


So, I was at the mission, the mission has a big outfit up there. I can't find the pictures now, it's too hard to find.

So tearin' down the old buildin's, the old Hudson Bay Factory in 1702, some fella made a bit of a diary book, a little list and he put it in the crack in the wall and it got shoved in and they found it when they tore the buildin' apart. And of course, he said in 1702 it was very hard times. He said there was not a thing movin', there was nothin'. He said it was terrible. Two or three would come along and they would take up possession of a family and they would kill them and they would stay there 'til they eat the meat all off that family and then go someplace else. It told about a woman suckin' her wee baby and she killed the baby and eat it. That's in 1702. So, you see such times as there's been. We hear nothin', and there's lots we'll never hear about.


I know what a talkie is because I heard it over here in the mission basement. Before that you had to read it off. They put the picture and you had to read about it. Be before your day. Now they talk as they're doin' it.

And my mother's mother, she says, "Rachel, I would like to see a picture show."

"My, goodness, mother, you're gettin' young in your old days."

"Well," she says, "I want to see a picture show."

Now she died at ninety-three and she had never seen a picture show up 'til then and my Grandmother and Grandfather Saunders, they never had a picture show that I ever knowed of. And my mother, she was very seldom at a picture show, and my other aunts, as far as I know. But my grandmother (on my mother's side, an old English woman and she died at 93, my mother died at 92), she wanted to see the show. They were in Owen Sound and my mother was keepin' boarders. They went to the picture show way up on that side of the market square in Owen Sound. It was ten cents I think. That's years ago. But you had to read it. It wasn't talkie stuff in them days.

So, my mother said to her mother, "Well, how did you like it?" "Oh," she says, "not too bad." Mother says, "Was it anything like what you thought it would be?" She says, "I had no idea what it would be like. But I wanted to see one picture show . . ." before she died. Isn't that awful, eh? One picture show before she died. Now they've got TV and lookin' at pictures all the time.


So that's just how I'm livin' here and puttin' in my old days. And the mission is my next of kin. If I get sick or hurt, they're supposed to bury me. Not leave me around for the dogs to bite at.

# Two Sisters

## On the Road from Cobalt to Haileybury

This is the loveliest corner you want to live in. I'll be sorry when I leave it. This corner is what I love.

I done what I could. Worked 'til I was seventy. A plain life but it's a nice life as long as I can live and make both ends meet. We pay cash for everything we get. I mean to say, I live according to my means.

Me and my sister—she was in the Val Gagnons fire when they went down in the ravine and all got smothered—we like to live the old-fashioned way. Wood and coal. It's company to have a stove in the house, warming yourself around the stove, but it's quite a job firing it up.

We have a bottle of brandy in the winter but we never drink outside the house.

I done all my beans, potatoes, pumpkins, beets, onions, carrots. The turnips aren't up yet.

We watch Peyton Place at six o'clock twice a week and The Edge of Night at half-past three. We've been watching them so long I can always remember.

We're old people. We never get rid of work, we accumulate it, but we never stop to think we're getting old.

Here it's so nice and quiet. You don't need to be afraid of anything. It's God's country.

# Phil Lepage

"At times, the stories don't seem to come, but other times it comes good. I can start and tell them for hours. I used to be a pretty good round dancer and I'd get up and watch for a fair lady that was a good dancer. They used to wear bustles. Anyway, I spied this girl and so away we went, goin' round the floor pretty slick, and all at once I seen a streak of sawdust fallin'. So I stopped and said, 'Pardon me, lady. I knewed very well that you had a waterpower there but I didn't think you had a sawmill built on it'."

He liked that story, and so had the nurses at the Haileybury hospital the week he'd been in to have a bone fixed in his neck, and he was saying that was one of the better times in his life, to talk to those two women. I was blushing. There was much more to the man than I'd expected; you could tell women amused him even now, the way they'd changed since he could remember, cut their hair, wore short dresses, got the vote, and smoked.

"And peoples asked me if I was ever married and I says, 'Sure, many times outside the church but never in it.' I've told that answer more than once, to those two womens, too."

He got up for his tea, pouring a pot of hot water into a soup bowl, sitting again, spooning it down, rescuing the tea bag for his afternoon cup. Now, if I was to give him a boot of tobacco, he'd try a pipeful for fun; he'd never seen that kind in the seventy years he'd smoked.

He poked it down the corncob and I thought about that morning and of the two men who told me about this fellow called Phil LePage. When they said he was a hundred, I'd been afraid to go because of his age and his frailty. They were sure he'd be at home, for he had no place to go. Home was up the road by Elk Lake Lodge.

I'd found the shack, just where the road turned back to town, grey boards nailed lengthwise into the tar paper to keep it from curling. There was one path from the door and it led to an outhouse ten feet back with a clothesline stretching along the distance. The door to the small shed had been opened, hooked to the inside wall, and on the same crossbeam, nailed five feet above the dirt floor, were his tools: a handsaw, a log-cutter and two hammers. To the right was another door, opening into a second room not more than twelve feet square.

White steam boiling up from a pot on the cooker had clouded the two windows so that the light in the room was grey, layered, and the air smelt of tobacco more than old age. I remember thinking there wasn't much in the room but the man. He was big for his age, with broad shoulders and wide hands, his army pants, pressed and suspended with police braces, giving him the same fit they had forty years before. He'd been playing cards, the same ones he now shuffled absently, twisted and turned from too many games of solitaire.

He was saying he did all his own washing. "I've no water but I've got a heavetrough and a barrel outside. Takes me one pail a week. I always was independent and I'm still are."

The electricity he'd put in two years ago interfered somehow with the life he'd been used to, and it was only switched on for the Wednesday and Saturday shave and the radio news at noon. The light bulb was never on; he said he was in bed before the sun.

He reckoned I couldn't imagine what goes through a man's head, lying awake at night on that iron cot in the far corner, thinking about everything, the good times. In the same corner, above the bed on hooks were a grey jacket and a blue suit still in its cellophane bag. It had been hanging under the cellophane since the nineteenth day of December last year, his birthday, and lord knows, he said, when it would be put on again. The grey one he wore to funerals.

The room was organized, almost spartan, the linoleum floor swept bare, his dustpan, broom and washbasin nailed, chest-high, to the wall by the two-burner stove, beside a small shelf he'd built for his plate, knife and fork. He claimed to be a good cook, pretty heavy though on macaroni, spaghetti and stews. Ten potatoes a day and rhubarb for breakfast. He'd leave turkey, or any meat for that matter, for beaver. It was knowing how to stew it right. Take every bit of fat off of it. Soak it in salt and water overnight. Parboil it with onions.

He liked those onions though they made him dream like the mischief. They'd fry up with skunk, groundhog and porcupine (now that's meat only good in the spring, when they've eaten some grass). Muskrat wasn't bad if it wasn't too dry and there was nothing like the hind-quarter of a lynx.

Nope, he'd never been lonely. Didn't know what loneliness was. Never had any fear and never had a day of school because it had been nine miles from the Pembroke farm where he was born, but he could read, learnt it himself from looking at the *Nugget* and the *Toronto Daily Star*. And he could still read a little with a spyglass, detectives and westerns mostly, but not for very long, so the winters pass more slowly now.

He kept the glass on the windowsill along with a straight razor, stolen from a dead German's packsack. For sixty years he'd shaved with that razor, putting it aside only when his hands got too shaky. And the three stick-pin poppies, well, he kept them just for the memories he could no longer share at the Legion. He was the last of the World War I veterans in town, and the oldest, he'd been told, in the country.

Never been broke, but lovely god, he could dream about it. Sometimes, he said, he'll haul off a fist or a foot, lying facing the wall, and then down he'd be on the floor with the blankets and everything, worked up because he'd dreamt he'd been caught in a strange place without money. He was an awful man to dream and he couldn't understand it, but he was with dead people a lot. There's not a week goes by he didn't relive the old times, talking with his dad about all the things he never said as a young boy, his father having died when he was nineteen.

His mother had been Irish and his father half-French and half-Irish, which made him, he figured, three-quarters Irish and one quarter French. His mind liked to work that way, in percentages, in orderly patterns. His day always began at half-past five.

> get up and straighten the blanket
> have a wash
> comb my hair
> get my cup ready for tea
> sit back on the bed and have a couple of pipefuls
> then open the door.

It was ten minutes short of noon and I asked him about death. He didn't care. They could come and get him any time. He had had only two wishes and one was to see a hundred. The only one left now was to pass away in that bed of his. He wouldn't mind that at all. They'd have to break in, 'cause he always locked his door at night, but people'd know something was wrong if the outside door wasn't open in the morning.

"Sure, if I could have write I would have had a real good dialogue."

He began that afternoon to tell me why.


This here is not a story, it's the true facts, but I don't like goin' over it. Well, if you want to hear I'll tell you. That's when I left home, in 1898. I had somewheres around $300 on me. That was big money at that time, believe me. So I intended to see somethin' and I travelled through 'til I got to Calgary, that's way out west.

I got off there and went into a hotel. Used to go in and have a drink now and again, but not too often. I went to the bartender and asked him for a drink of scotch. He poured a glass and one of the bums on the side of me gaffled it. So I said to the bartender, "Get me another." He poured me another but there was a bum on the other side and he thought this fellow had got off easy and he went to do the same. So I just nailed him and caught the other fellow and both of them dropped. I had a pair of arms on me at that time and there wasn't many who could handle them. And there were a couple more of their friends who wanted to butt in, so I used the foot a little, 'cause there was too many of them. Anyway, I cleaned up.

There was a bunch of fellas standin' back, all dressed as cowboys with spurs on them and all. One of them come up to me and said, "Say, can you ride a horse?" I says sure, I was born down on a farm and we used to ride bareback all over the fields. "You won't have to ride bareback here. We've got a good pony and saddle for you," he says.

I thought maybe they were ranchers, maybe they'll take me out and I'll have a job. So I says, okay. We went out to the shed and they all had horses and there was a spare one. "There's your pony." I went over and patted it a little and seen it was a very friendly horse. "Hop on, we'll ride out." I says all right and we pulled out and up the railroad track quite a piece from Calgary. Took a trail up the mountain. Well, I says to myself, maybe their ranch is way up there, so I'll go up. We got up quite a piece and we got into a little place, there was a nice little brook runnin'. Oh, quite a beaver hut in there and they had that for a corral. They left their ponies hobbled so they couldn't get away.

We walked up a piece further and we got into the gang, some of them playin' cards. They were all fixed with two big guns, one on each side. So this fella introduced me to the boss. He says, "We've got a new partner." "Oh, that's good," the boss says, "Rig him up." He went away and got me a big beltful of shells and two guns, one for each side. "Jeepers," I says, "what's comin' on?" "Well," he says, "to initiate you tonight, we've got to rob a train down here." It was them Dalton Boys. You've maybe read about them. There've been books on them. An outlaw gang, that's what I had runned into. Oh, I says to myself, I daren't run away, 'cause they'll shoot me.

That night we pulled down just about ready for the train. Went down and stopped the train. There was s'pposed to be a big payroll on the train but it wasn't on. It had went ahead. We got quite a little money all right, but not the big payroll. One of our fellas got killed. We had them stop the train and disconnect the engine and take it ahead a little piece. They'd gone to break into the mail car and that's when one of the fellas got shot. Of course, the mail guy got shot right off of the bat. They took what they figured was the registered mail.

Anyway, we got back to camp. There was about $3,000 and that was a generous split amongst the bunch. We lay down low for two or three days and then we went across to the States. Not very far from the state line there, we went off and robbed a bank. Nobody hurt. We met Jesse James and his bunch. They were goin' one way and we were goin' the other. Just bid the time of day. So we come back up and robbed 'bout three different banks, none of them in Canada.

Later I had made up my mind, I got to get. That's all there was to it. I figured I may be one of them to get shot or somethin'. One night I caught a little bit of iron rations. We just rolled our saddle blankets and slept at the foot of a tree here and there in the summertime. So I made sure I was off toward the trail the furtherest, near a nice big tree that was there. We always had a bonfire at night and this time, when the fire got down pretty well, you could hear one snorin', and another one, and then all over. There was fourteen of us there when I left them.

When they were all asleep, I thought the best thing I can do is take my chance. I unbuckled my belt and left the two guns right there. I wouldn't take any. If they catch me anyplace, I'll be unarmed anyway. I got down and caught the pony and I led him down the hill 'til we got to the track. But I was cute enough I wouldn't follow the track, 'cause if you follow it they could follow your footprints. I went on the edge of the bush.

I followed down, comin' east toward the east. I says I'll get as far as I can 'til daylight, then I'll quit if I can find a brook. I did too. It was just gettin' daylight and I got into a little place with a brook runnin'. I went up the brook a piece and there was a nice beaver dam. I un-saddled the pony and hobbled him so he wouldn't get away and lay down under a tree there and slept all day.

That evenin' when it started to get dark, away I went. Before daybreak, I ran into a tank where the train takes water along the track. One of those big tanks. I says by golly, this is a dandy chance here to catch a freight train. So I pulled the saddle off of the pony. I didn't hobble him that day, I let him go, "You take your luck", and left the saddle near the tank.

It wasn't very long, the train come headin' for the east. I watched round there while they were takin' water and seen an empty car and I jumped in. Rode for two weeks and got off at Mattawa, Ontario. I knewed it was a lumberjack town and I thought I'd let on that I was lookin' for work, goin' to let on that I was broke.

So I walked downtown to the hotel, the Mattawa House, and I says to the proprietor that I was lookin' for work and that I'm broke. "All right", he says, "we'll give you a room here. We'll be sending men every other day or so up to the camp. Just go into the dining room and have your meals. I said okay. Of course, I wasn't takin' a drink at all. I kept quiet. But I had over $3,000 on me. I'd got it from the raids we'd made.

In two days, off I went to the lumber camp and I stayed there right through to the drive and I stayed there to boom and right through the season.

I stayed up there all summer, workin' on a farm 'til the camp come in again in the fall, and went back to the logging camp. Put in the whole winter and the next spring too.

That next summer I stayed around Mattawa for about two months. And there was dances about every second night out in the country. I got acquainted with a lot of the girls and a lot of the boys and we used to take a bottle of liquor and we'd rent a buggy. They'd charge three dollars a night for the buggy and the horse and of course, we were only supposed to be two but, as the general rule, we always had each a girl and we'd get the girls to start off a little and we'd catch them on the way out of town. We done that all summer.

I was around there 'til nineteen-seven. Then I come up to Elk Lake in August and that's sixty-four years this month. A fella from Mattawa, he was workin' a bunch of claims up at Silver Lake and he got after me to come here. It was better than a lumber camp. We got two dollars and a half a day and our board. That was a whole lot better than $30 a month. I worked out at Silver Lake for eighteen months and I quit and got into the TR mine on the Gowganda road. I was around here workin' in mines right through 'til I enlisted. Went down to Haileybury and enlisted and drilled there for a while 'til we got transferred to Niagara and formed the 37th Battalion.

They called for the draft of the 17th Reserve and a bunch of my friends and I wanted to get on it. We managed to get on and away, sailed and went to England. I was lucky 'cause I got in with some of the fellows. You know in the army, there's not many of them that's got money. Well, I was carryin' pretty good. On the way we were playin' this housey-housey, which is bingo today, and I made quite a little on the boat goin' across. And I won the log twice. When I got to England I had quite a little bunch of money.

They put me on escort duty for a while there. Just a few days before the 2nd Division sailed for France, they called for a bunch of volunteers. You see, the 17th Reserve was a reserve battalion. They kept them there for reinforcing, they told me. I volunteered but they said I could go on the 15th, an Ontario battalion. I said nothin' doin'. They wear kilts and I'm not a woman to wear kilts. So they said there's the 25th, the Nova Scotia Battalion. Do they wear pants? Okay, I'll jump onto that one. We sailed to France and stayed with them right through the war to Halifax.

I was way past forty at the time of the First World War. I could get away easy 'cause I was a volunteer. In the trenches, over the top and all over, I was right through all Vimy Ridge. One of the swellest battles the Canadians ever took. The French people tried and lost 70,000 people. England lost over 100,000 soldiers and they couldn't take it. Us Canadians, only a handful, walked clean over with it.

We went three lines at a time before they ever opened fire. They had been on their guard right through and word come down to them that night, to them not us, that everything was called off. Then, of course, the whole bunch of Germans went asleep and they didn't know what happened. We were on the third line of their defence before they heard our artillery or anything open.

On the way down to Vimy Ridge, we caught the big staff officers in great big dugouts, caught them in their pyjamas, caught the whole goddamn bunch of them. They looked right at home with their electric lights but they weren't at home that morning! I was put on a stretcher party and I was carryin' wounded and we done that the rest of the day.

That night we were relieved, other ones took our places. We had lost awful heavy, but where we lost the most was at the Somme. We went in there 1,140 and we came out 82 of us. Took her back two weeks, got filled up again, went back full strength, came back 202. I was one of the luckiest ones in both raids, never got a scratch. Just a touch of the gas once. You had to watch sometimes. They blewed it out of tanks. See, with a very, very slow wind they'd open the gas up. Any wind that was comin' our way, they'd open the tanks and they'd blow out easy. You had to watch. It was treacherous. The wind would happen to change and it would turn back sometimes.

A man watched all the time. You could see it comin' just like a yellow dust, comin' very slow. This time there was three of us. I had stolen a jar of rum and there was a captain and a sergeant major with me. We'd got into a cellar in this French town and we'd been drinkin' pretty heavy. This time it was this mustard gas that they shot over. They shoot that in the shell, the shell falls and she just breaks open. Of course, we didn't wake up to put our masks on. We didn't hear the gas alarm and it was a little late when we got it. So the officer, he come to and shook us. We were lucky 'cause we were full of rum or we'd a been gone. But it affected me for some time after I got back. I can feel it every now and again.

The armistice was signed on the eleventh of November. We were in Germany quite a piece then. We couldn't travel very fast because we had to give the German army time to move ahead of us and get out. We followed them. I was just on the outskirts of Mons when the armistice was signed. We were told the night before. They said tomorrow at eleven o'clock the armistice was goin' to be signed. Oh, there was very little shootin' done, hardly any at all. And the next mornin' at eleven, a little piece away, there was a machine-gun nest of Germans and at eleven o'clock they got up out of the pit and yelled, "Good-bye Canadians". Talkin' English, just as plain English as they could get it.

They started off with the machine guns and started back. That night we walked into Mons. We were in one part of Mons and they were in the other. They kept on movin'. We were there a few days.

Then we got into a French town, a real big city. We were the first Canadians to go there. And you talk about somethin' desperate! They broke the ranks, womens and olden people. They'd come up and pull you out of the ranks. Some of them had wine and liquor and things. When we got to the square, the officer said, "Well, I guess we don't need to look for no billets." They were sayin' there's a bed at their place. And there's a bed for two or three, and in no time the whole bunch was discarded.

They trimmed us of everything, every badge and even some of the buttons on the tunic was all cut off for souvenirs. We were there a week. They had to send back to get buttons and badges.

By god, that night we were all into a big theatre, a hell of a big theatre and they was dancin' and dishin' cognac and geneva. That's gin, the only kind of liquor, but that was free. You'd see the womens dancin' with the officers' hats on and an officer with maybe a woman's hat on his head. Oh, you talk about a real time, lovely god. The reeve of the town, he was a real old man and he got on the stand there and he told his people, "Now here are the fair Canadians and they're the ones that delivered us. Give them your wives if they want them!" An oldish, white-headed man and he was sayin, "Give them your wives if they want them." Lovely god, nobody had to look for billets there.

Then we left and went ahead quite a little bit more. Before we crossed into Germany, right on the border, there was a little potato patch and we happened to see a wild boar and we got him and roasted the whole works.

I was a sniper. Snipin' and scoutin'. We were always in some place where nobody could see you, fixed up in a place that was raised a little, and always an officer with you and fieldglasses. Some of those rifles carry a mile and a half, two miles. One time, there was a German officer, he was off the line a little piece. My officer spied him. I took a good bead on him and the officer told me I got him. Word got back that it was one of the real high officers and I was mentioned in the *Dispatch* that week.

One time there was an awful lot of rounds of fire. A bunch of wild geese goin' across. Oh, you should 'ave heard the shootin'. Some of them with machine guns. There was two of them come down, but across the line. We didn't get any. They fell across the line and the Germans got them. Lovely god, there was a lot of ammunition fired that day.


After the war I sailed with the 25th Nova Scotia Battalion right to Halifax. We got paid there and I had $932.20. They paid me right there in spot cash but I didn't get my discharge. I got a paper to get in civvy clothes. The next day, which was Sunday, we were pullin' out. There was a special train, two hundred and forty of us that didn't belong to Halifax. There was some goin' clean right through to Vancouver. I had to change in Montreal and go through by Toronto. I got in on Tuesday mornin' and my train north pulled out at nine at night. While I was waitin' I bought civvy clothes, a dandy black suit, but I stayed in my uniform. Took the train to North Bay and then to Earlton.

When we got out was there ever a bunch at the station. They had the banners and the school kids singin'. They had one fella playin' the flute and the other playin' a big brass drum to meet some of us. None of them knew I was comin' 'cause I didn't tell no one.

There was a young lady right below and she shouted, "Mother, look at who's here;" and in one jump she was right on the platform, caught me by the neck and give me a kiss. I took her for another girl. Of course, when I got down the mother was right there and I knew who she was as soon as I seen the mother. She had grewed quite a little, four years and eight months away.

Then we was shakin' hands and it took us a little while. We all paraded down to the Legion hall along with the schoolchildren. The young girl was walkin' with me.

After the war I come back to Elk Lake and I've been here ever since. Worked for the Department of Highways for a while, then I quit and went with the Foresters. In the winter I trapped. In the spring, go back out. Then I sold the trap ground and retired. But I was past my age before I ever got a pension but the Legion got after me. So I took the pension. I get $80 for the old age pension and $81 from the veterans' pension. That gives $161 a month. I can live like a king with that. I'm well satisfied.

These people ask me what the secret is fer livin' over a hundred, so I say I never smoked a cigarette in my life and you got to be easy with women and go to bed early at night. And then they ask if I had my life over again what would I do. I says I'd do the same as what I did.

# Kenabeek Gothic

We took to farming and all the neighbours would come to give a
hand to clear your land. Logging bees we called them. We'd set a table
of meat, potatoes, vegetables, cakes and pies and pies and cakes. In
the early days you didn't need drink to entertain.

And then in the spring when the suckers were runnin', we used to
have canned fish. Those were good days, but you wouldn't want to go
back.

The only real trouble we've had was when the Haileybury fire
swept through, drove moose and bear and deer into our field and Jim
had rode the horses that week with his head stuck in a barrel of water.

# Bella Armstrong
## A Miner's Wife

There was something tough and northern about Bella. Those eyes could freeze you to granite if you started meddling in her affairs. She'd been living in that same house in Cobalt for forty years, and to her meddling was knocking on the white wood door with the Hugh and Bella Armstrong sign. Meddling was wanting to sit and talk in the kitchen when she still had two weeks of washing to feed to the wringer.

But her husband had opened the door and let me in. He was a quiet man, stooped from the mines, burnt-out somehow over the years. He had a small piece of silver on him, the size of a fingernail, which he tapped on the table, trying to remember the mines he'd been down. Bella was pretty poor at keeping to herself, circling the kitchen, to the stove and back to the washer, circling with the eye of a den mother.

It was late afternoon before she spoke, telling me I was to stay for tea. She was iron-proud, but the eyes had warmed a shade and you could tell she figured I'd earned my stay. She was careful to take the stool on the other side of the table, slicing down the banana bread, never moving from the upright position, determined to keep her old back perpendicular.

So yer from down there, eh. Well, I'm 83 past and he's 88. He was born in Nipissing where there's a little village backed in. Nipissing Village, that's where he's registered and that's where his baptism is. It's a village though, 'cause it never was a town.

99

When he first come up to Cobalt in 1905, there was a few tents, a few shacks. When I come in 1909, it was a busy place. There was lots of stores and people, all dressed down. There was no such thing as goin' naked. And you know that was the days when they had those great big hats with the plumes on it. They had corsets too, but I couldn't wear them 'cause my hips was too small. I was bigger round here than ever the hips.

No, this place will never be a ghost town. It's known worldwide. Back then, it wasn't so much Eaton's but we had all kinds of grocery stores and there was Syrians and Greeks. Lots of Chinese. Lots of laundries. One man came fer me in the night with a wagon, nothin' on it but the seat, and that's the way I went in the night fer a baby to be born. And I went on the bunks of a sleigh another time. Sure you do things. You have to do them. You don't say no. You just do them.

This couple weren't married to each other, they were livin' together and the fellow, he come in the mornin' to get me 'cause his baby was to be born. Well, she went through quite a lot before the baby came and out it did come in the end. When it did come, I don't know what she did but with every heartbeat there seemed to be a gush of blood comin' from her and I thought, What am I goin' to do? How can I stop it?

So I run home and got an old cotton sheet. They had a kind of old-fashioned stove and I tore the sheet in strips about so wide and I scorched them on the stove and I packed her with that myself. I done that and then I raised the foot of the bed up on a chair. I didn't know what else to do.

Try it, try it. Try a little native. Some of those things should be told. There's not many of them left now that experienced them kind of things.

Sure, we had hard times, eh. When I think back over it what I hate worse when I think of those things is them darn maggots. That all happened in the bush, those experiences, that's where I had them.

When old Mrs. Sebelt died, they sent for me and they come with the lumber wagon and you sit on the board across the seat. You know what a lumber wagon is? It's a big heavy wagon. Steel rims, ruckety-rook, ruckety-rook. I had to take Sonny with me, that's my oldest boy, he was only six months. Had to take him with me, six or seven in the morning. I took him 'cause I breast-fed my babies.

Well then, they wouldn't give me nothin' to put on her but a night-gown. Wouldn't give me one of her dresses. That's the way they did in England, apparently. We carried her downstairs, the two girls and I,

one fourteen and one sixteen. We carried her down but the stairs was crooked and we had to do it before she got cold and too stiff, eh.

The next one I had a girl commit suicide and it was in the heat, the end of June. I went to call in there and I laid her out and fixed her up 'til they come with the casket. The undertaker came and just put her in the casket and they brought in a doctor but it was never investigated or anything. She was in the casket but they never covered her. She should have had a cover 'cause she blew all up, her lips went blue, and she just wilted. And she was pregnant, that's why she done it. And she just blew up, it was terrific.

Her husband, he was a deserter and was off somewhere in the bush but the fellow who fathered this here child went out and got drunk and it was a couple of days before he came back and found that body layin' there. Well, the flies flew on it and it got all maggoty and they sent fer me. And I had to come and wash them darn big maggots, all round her neck, her hair, her ears. Her ears were full. I washed her and I try to think back of what I used in the water. I think it musta been vinegar, 'cause vinegar is kind of an acid. Vinegar and water. Had to wash and dug her ears out. But you know, I didn't get them all out. And the smell of her when they were takin' her to the grave.

I was twenty-five years old, that's how old I was. I don't think I realized some of the danger I was put in. I just done it 'cause it was there to be done.

One time, I went and the doctor was there all right. It was kind of an abortion, I think. My gosh, that must have been four or five months, that baby. I can still see it. Worked all night and when they brought it, it was kind of cute, eh, and you know what the doctor did with that? They had a box, a coal stove, one of them round ones, and he put that in there and burnt it, right in the house. No medication.

I never thought couldn't I or could I before I did it. I didn't know enough to say I can't do it. Saw what was to be done and I did it. What your eyes see impels you to do it, eh?

Bella poured herself another cup of tea, in the silence of the room. She'd said what she had to say, and now she wanted to forget.

No, I never was a suffragette, neither do I believe in this equalization of women or some darn thing. They got the upper hand of them now if they'd only realize it.

I read this book called *Before Adam* that said we come from a sort of apes, that we descended from that. That was the idea. It showed about the apes and all what's goin' on befores, eh, and how they learnt first to put two trees together and lash them with bark fer to cross a stream. These apes don't want to be wet. We elevated from that.

That was one of the things to show that at one time we were on all fours. Now, you watch the boys and girls of today, they have their hair hangin' down, none of them straighten up, none of them throw their shoulders back. Now that's this generation. The next generation is goin' to be a little more bent over. But the fourth generation is goin' back on all fours unless they straighten up. I won't be here to see it, but it will be.

# Moonshine

## "You Can Make Your Own Heaven and Hell Right Here on the Ground"

20 pounds sugar
1 pint real lemon juice
1 gallon water
Bring to boil
Simmer for half-hour
Add 8 gallons warm water
Cool at 110 degrees
Ferment one month at 60 degrees
Distil at one ounce per minute at 174 degrees
Will yield two gallons of 160 percent proof
Sterilize everything

# Alec Pope

Alec Pope liked his whiskey. And he'd tell you that whether it was home brew or government stuff or what the devil, as long as there was a kick to it, it could keep a body alive. Why, half a bottle last year saved him from dying of the flu. Worst sickness he'd had in thirty years. The only other time he'd been sidelined was when he hit a rotten tree too quickly and the axe slipped and sliced his instep. Got laid up for months, and to keep from going crazy he'd painted deer and moose on that kitchen wall, the one just over his shoulder. That's how the mural got there.

Oh, he'd done all right he figured. Bought this big house, paid for it out of beaver skins. Sold out a few mining claims but never went south to spend it. Never went crooked like some of the prospectors he knew. Good god, he wouldn't live in the city, everybody rushing here and there for a nickel or ten cents, trying to do one another. Give him the bush and the wilds, you're more contented, you're free, that's all a person wants in this world.

Pope's glass was never empty that morning. He was a great man to talk, or maybe it was the Irish in him. Whatever, he'd created his own legend in that part of the country, stories that turned up in pubs and snack bars forty miles in every direction. I first heard about Pope back in Elk Lake, and that's how I got to be in Gowganda that day, a small bush town on a lake where Pope says you can fish your head off and you won't get a bite. The blooming tourists have skinned the country.

I'd found his place at the top of the hill on the north shore, a big white clapboard house on a large butt of granite rock. He'd been packing up to go for a day of blasting rock and prospecting down at Shining Tree, but insisted on staying, cracking open a bottle of Crown Royal, checking to see if the tape recorder was running before he sat down, as he was now, his long legs stretched under the table and his pipe in hand, telling me just how it used to be.

It's all been happy for me. The whole bloomin' business. I've enjoyed myself ever since I came to Canada.

My mother was a very stiff Roman Catholic. We were all brought up that way, all eight of us. My father, he was a Protestant and he had this big business in Ireland, the wine and spirit trade, in the city of Waterford. He used to make a lot of whiskey and ship it over to Scotland where it was aged. He was awfully rich and we had a big estate there and with everything under the sun. I used to go to school, to the old Jesuit fathers. They're a very militant part of the Roman Catholic church.

My mother had a sister up in Dublin. She was a great big woman and stern, very disciplined, and she had a great big private hospital there. She always liked nursing, so she bought her own hospital. Mother wanted me to go up to Dublin and get in the school of art, 'cause I always liked to sketch. So I went and stayed with this old aunt. I didn't get along with her too well, I guess, 'cause she thought she'd make a priest out of me.

At the time, the old Archbishop of Ireland thought he was goin' to die and came to Molly's (my aunt) hospital. I don't know what he had, cancer or what the devil. They had to operate on him and before they put the ether to him he said to Molly that he'd grant her any request she put to him if she got him through. So the operation was a success. The old jigger was all right. And then she asked him to make a priest out of me.

I'd been an altar boy, used to go to confession when I didn't know any better. But I got kinda fed up with that. This old priest would slide the door open and ask all kinds of personal questions. How the family was, how my father was goin' to vote and how my mother was goin' to vote.

Anyway, Molly got her wish, sort of. I went to a place called Nava, sixty miles south of Dublin. That's where this great big copper, nickel and zinc mine is now. I put in four years there at the seminary. They were all Jesuits too, learnin' Latin and Greek and all the rest of the stuff I had no use for.

When I came home the last year my dad asked me if I was goin' to be ordained. "Nothin' doin'," I says, "I wouldn't spend my life with a bunch of blackguards like that." You could imagine what was goin' on in those dormitories at nighttime there. They were all men. Shockin'. That fed me up with the whole outfit. So dad asks me what I wanted to do. "Would you like to join the navy, go to Australia or any place you'd like?"

I headed for Canada.


I was seventeen when I came across on the boat. My dad gave me some money to start out and I came through to Toronto and there was a friend of my father's there who ran a hotel. Flannigan was his name. These were hard times, hard to get a job, so I asked old Flannigan. I gave him a letter of introduction and some testimonials as far as my character went.

"Yah," he said, "I know your father. We went to school together, but I can't give you a job round the hotel. Wages round here aren't too good but we'll find you a start someplace. I'll send you down to a company that makes these stained glass windows." So I got in there. They had a big table with all these different colour glass and design and I had to fit them all in, lead them round and solder. I stayed at that for about a week.

I boarded up in town for some three dollars a week. There was an old fella there, he was a great big man, lazy, an Englishman. He just sat in a chair all day and he used to send me down to the bar with a couple of galvanized pails and I'd get each one filled for twenty-five cents with beer. He paid it and I'd bring them up and he'd just sit there and drink. Everyday it was the same when I came back from work.

Then I heard of the Cobalt rush, it was nearly finished at the time. I was goin' north anyway, me and my partner. There was quite a little activity when we got there. I didn't know anything about minerals, if I had I coulda been a millionaire today. My partner disappeared into the bush someplace with an outfit and I heard the call fer to go further north. Git yerself a homestead and you're independent for life. A hundred and sixty acres, you get it free from the government and you got to clean the land yourself. So I came up to a place called Charlton, just north of Englehart and I located a hundred and sixty acres way up the head of Long Lake and I cleared eleven acres there by hand, just tore the bush down and grubbed all the stumps out and put in the crop. Oats, potatoes. Oh, virgin ground, the stuff was six feet deep but you couldn't get any market for the crops. So they just rotted in the ground and I used what I could out of them. In the wintertime I used to trap. Then I got on to studyin' rocks and I got prospectin' and I've been prospectin' ever since.

It was in October and five inches of snow came right on top of us. And everybody just living in tents, tarpaulins and one thing and another. The government sent in a whole bunch of those streetcars, and we used to live in them. That fire in 1922 swept the whole country. My first wife was down at Charlton when the big fire came through and I was up in the bush. I hiked out ahead of the flames and got down to Charlton. There was a powerhouse there, a big cement powerhouse, and there was two hundred people in there, and she was there. And five babies were born that night and she was the nurse. She looked after the whole five babies. Right out in the open they had the kids, that place was crammed full. The woodwork on the windows looked glowing red, scorched, but they didn't burn completely, they held together. And the smoke didn't get in. That's what saved all the people.

You look from one side of the town to the other and all you could see was a stovepipe stickin' up here and there and a dead pig and a dead horse, chickens and everything else all over the place burnt up. Went right through to Haileybury and Liskeard.

Down Liskeard there, they all got in the Roman Catholic church and the old father said this won't burn, this won't burn and he sanctified it and everything else. Hell, she burned down just the same. He couldn't save it with all his cantations. Couldn't save it.

Ruth, my daughter, she was ready to go to school, so I had to leave the land and come back to Charlton and get a house.

Ruth was eight when her mother died (she used to take epileptic fits) and I was away at the time trappin' in the bush and somebody brought me news that my wife had died that night. She took a fit in bed and turned right round and smothered to death in the pillow.

Then Dominion Explorers heard of me bein' a prospector (they were a big outfit that were goin' up to stake claims and survey the Arctic for minerals) and they asked me if I'd go up there. Sure, I jumped at the chance. Ruth stayed in Charlton while I was up in the Arctic five seasons with the Eskimos.

When I left Charlton to go up to the Arctic that first time, they never told me from Toronto what I had to get. So I got myself two suits of the heaviest wool clothing, a coat and pants, scotch wool and all black. I got my ticket to go to Edmonton and then I was supposed to go north on the train as far as it went up to a place called Fort McMurray. They said I'd meet a fella there by the name of Bill Brooch, he's flyin' one of these machines, big Fairchilds. So I got up there in due time, 'bout three days, and stayed the first night and met this Bill Brooch. He was a real rough old jigger. An awful man to drink, playin' poker every night.

But, however, I went down to the plane in the morning. He saw me comin' in my black suit with this old eiderdown. He says, "You're goin' north with me today." He was staggerin' all over. I thought, by god, you're a fine lookin' man to fly. I didn't give a rip anyway. He put two big fifty-gallon drums of gas in the plane and threw a bunch of groceries and mail in the back and there wasn't any more room than three feet to the fuselage.

He says, "Get in."

I says, "Where?"

"Right on top of those barrels there. Lay on your belly up there."

I squeezed in (my back was touchin' the top of the plane) and I laid flat right over those barrels, and right over his head down in the cockpit. He got the engine goin' and started down the runway. Just as he was leavin' the ice to take to the air, I heard a snap, a quick snap. He never noticed and she took off anyway. It was a nice bright day and not a breath of wind. I'd read a little 'bout airplanes and knew the different parts so I was watchin' him.

We got to 6,000 feet and 'bout a hundred and fifty miles from Fort McMurray when the engine conked, sputtered and backfired. He just reached over and turned on the other tank. But it was then I noticed the wing of the plane swingin' back and forth. I looked at the other side and there wasn't a move in it.

The bolt that goes through the plane musta broken off when we were leavin', and if there'd been any wind at all, we'd have crashed. This old wing was open and swingin' about eight inches. He never noticed it and I thought there's no use in sayin' a darn word, she's flyin' all right. He might just of got panicky and down we'd have went for sure. He was pretty drunk and we had three hundred miles to go with that wing swingin' back and forth.

Then he says, "There she is". We were comin' to base camp. Just the tops of stovepipes stickin' out of the snow. He just got sober enough that he didn't land right away but circled slow 'til he came down on the beach. Well, the minute the plane hit the beach, away it threw me out the top about thirty feet. The plane turned all upside down and the barrels were rollin'. Brooch was thrown out the other side. We weren't a bit hurt or nothin'. He was a black lookin' jigger before we started, dark-skinned, but he'd turned as white as that there milk, and I started to laugh. I says, "What about the plane?" "Oh," he says, "forget it."

We went up to the camp and got into the rum, pretty tight. Then he asked me what happened and I told him 'bout this damn wing flyin'. He said, "Lovely . . ." and he started to swear. Then he says, "Why didn't you tell me?" I said if I'd have told him we'd 'ave been down in the barrens for god knows how long.

Well, he come over and threw his arms around me to kiss me. Tickled all to pieces.


It was my second day at base camp and, as I said, we'd been into the rum pretty good. Jack Rodgers, the head geologist, said, "Alec, will you take the Model T Ford and go down the beach there about a quarter of a mile away and put a couple of drums of gas on there and bring it up?" I says, "Sure." He says, "Can you drive a Model T?" I says, "Sure."

It had tracks on it, steel tracks. There'd been a big storm a couple days before and it had drifted everything level. The snow was just as hard as it could be. So I saw one track goin' down to the beach and I thought I'd better get on that. I started 'er up and got down this old track; hell, it was as hard as cement. I got off a little bit and it was just the same way. So I went down and put the two drums on and started back. And instead of keepin' on the road, I took another route I thought was a better way to get back into camp. There was six snow-houses there with Eskimos in them and they were all covered up, level on top, just a little hole on top where you could see maybe a wee bit of smoke comin' out. You'd never know there was an Eskimo in the damn place.

Well, I was drivin' along makin' a circle back to camp, when all of a sudden the whole Model T Ford took a dive down into one of these snowhouses. I broke through the roof, went right down among the damn Eskimos inside. How word travelled so quick I don't know, but there was about six or seven Eskimo houses under the snow, igloos, you know, drifted tight and they all come out through the holes in the front and the dogs came out and there was the dam'dest hullabaloo you ever saw in your life. And the lads in the camp all came runnin' out.

"Pope, you're crazy. Why didn't you keep on the old tracks?" I says I didn't know anything about it, I couldn't see a thing. And the old Model T Ford was right down in the middle of this snowhouse, right at the bottom. We had a heck of a time gettin' it out of there.


Those Eskimos, they're smart. They can do anything. You can take an old dollar watch and give it to one and he won't be satisfied 'til he pulls the whole thing apart to see how it works. He'll pull every nut and bolt and springs out of it and by tomorrow morning he'll have the whole thing together again, workin' perfect. 'Course, he never saw a watch in his life before. They're quick. Wonderful people.


There was three planes from Dominion Explorers which started out from Fort McMurray, that's at the head of Clear Water Creek, head of the Mackenzie River. They were taking Lajeunesse and I down to Aklavik to go in the mountains for the winter, all our supplies and everything.

The year before, Dominion Explorers had sent two men up the Nahanni River to prospect and stay the winter. When we got down to Fort McPherson, these fellows were supposed to have been out but they didn't come. So we tied up there for about three days. No sign of them.

So Bill Spence, the pilot, jumps in his plane and flies off up the Nahanni River. He spotted them comin' out with a dog team and a big tobogganful of stuff. Just two men. So after a while, they came across the far side of the river and over to the Hudson Bay post. One of them was the Mad Trapper. He was short, very dark skinned, dark hair. His partner was a tall, red-headed Scotchman. He had very little to say anyway.

They had this great big long sleigh with the dogs, a big tarp over it, bulging right out with all kinds of stuff. He come into the office of Dominion Explorers. They asked where his samples were. He said, "I've got no samples." "Well," they said, "what were you doin' back there all winter?" He says, "Trappin'".

They said they'd have to pay him for the time they hired him. "We sent you in there and we have to pay you your full time." Jack Rodgers gave him a check for about a thousand dollars. Then the Mad

Trapper pulls up his team in front of the Hudson Bay post and takes off the cover. My god, he had thousands of dollars' worth there of ermine, sable, beautiful skins. He sold them there for a heck of a pile of money. Then he went back up the Nahanni River again.

How he got into that section of the country and that part of the river was he came across from Dawson City and the Yukon. He trekked across the mountains and got this job prospectin' with Dominion Explorers. No one knew anything about him. Kind of a reserved fellow and very quiet, but a bad-lookin' actor. Carried his rifle with him every place he went.

So he went away back up the mountains and got meddlin' with some Indians' traps up there, stealin' fur and stealin' their traps on them. These Indians came out and reported to the Northwest Mounted Police and the police went after him. They chased him around quite a bit at the Mackenzie River and at last they saw him. This fellow had got both his feet frozen and was in bad shape. He used to walk on his snowshoes backward to fool the police.

However, he shot two of the police. That's the reason the Mounties were really after him then. They got him on the back of the Rat River (that's the river I used goin' up into the mountains), climbing the bank one day. He was headin' off some place and they shot him from the plane. And that was the end of him. I saw his grave the last time I was up there, just a shallow grave on the bank of the river with a wooden cross, that's all.

But he was a bad actor. He probably killed somebody over in Dawson City, 'cause when they went down and found him, he just had a little canvas bag and he had a little sewing outfit and a few cartridges and a full set of false teeth, top and bottom. They were gold, solid gold. A beautiful set of teeth.

I knew him. I saw him. I knew him well. When he come up to the Hudson Bay post I chummed around with him all afternoon, tryin' to find out stuff. But he wouldn't tell you anything. He was very reserved.


People in the city get afraid 'cause they read a bunch of junk. They believe in all they read. Some of these fellas s'pposed to be explorers, and they'll tell you the darndest stories and it's just a bunch of lies they make up. Especially about the Arctic. 'Cause the Arctic is all right. It's a tough place to live but there's nothin' wrong with it. You're just as safe there as you are here. As long as you have a gun and you don't get mixed up with a grizzly or a big brown bear.

And the Eskimo people are wonderful. They're the best on earth. I wouldn't ask for anybody any better. They'll do anything for you and they're smart. I used to go huntin' seal with them, killin' caribou and polar bear. Minerals all over the place, I'd be stakin' for Dominion Explorers. I had a great time up there if it wasn't fer the mosquitoes. They were somethin' terrible. You had to smear yourself with coal oil and lard all the time. I wore the same shirt up there for six months. No use in washin' it. You'd put it on and you had to put the grease on again, and you had to sleep with it that way.

I found some Iceland spar up there which was a very rare mineral (the war was on then, 1914) and I went up there with a partner from Cobalt by the name of Henry Lajeunesse. He was just a little, short fella, a prospector, though.

They put us way up in the mountains there, seventy-five miles north of Aklavik (that was at the mouth of the Mackenzie River). So we were seventy-five miles back in the mountains and we put in one winter there, the two of us in a tent. All we had was a little gasoline stove. I remember one night the bulb of the thermometer was half-full of mercury. It was pretty near ninety below zero. Cold, but we were dressed in caribou skins. We used to sleep in them.

We killed our own meat, all caribou. And they were up there by the millions. I've seen the skyline there pretty near black in the sun if the sun was goin' down. Never saw the like of it. We were always prowlin' around fer two or three hours in the day as long as there was daylight. In the wintertime, it's dark, it's just about like moonlight. The sun is so low and it's only up for an hour or so and then it pops down again and then the moon comes up and there's a kind of blue haze all over the snow. But you can see, you can see quite good.

And the snow was just as hard as cement. You can walk anyplace without snowshoes. I built an igloo there for real bad storms and we used to get in there 'cause the tent would be floppin' and raisin' the devil and you couldn't sleep, too much noise.

When I was comin' out one trip on the boat with Henry Lajeunesse, there was a woman by the name of Switzer. A little short woman with high boots on. She carried a gun on her belt and her packsack. We were waitin' for the boat at Aklavik when she landed in. She'd walked all the way from Dawson City right through the mountains to catch the boat and come out to civilization. And she got there 'bout three days before the boat was ready to go.

She got on board and Henry and I talked to her quite a bit. She was a traveller and quite a writer, doin' a lot of writin'. And that's all the gun she had, this pistol on her hip. She didn't give a rip about caribou, bears, or anything else. She used to camp out in her eiderdown, she had no tent.

So she was on the boat (it takes two weeks to come back up on the boat) and there was a fellow there by the name of Power. He was half-Negro and he'd been trappin' way up in the northern islands. He'd come down to Aklavik, sold his fur, and he wanted to get out to civilization. So he got on with this Miss Switzer and they got acquainted. Before we reached Fort McMurray at the end of the trip he was goin' to marry her the next winter. They got engaged anyway. The two of them came and asked me about Northern Ontario, what chances were there of settlin' down and gettin' a homestead. I said, "The best in the world. You can get all the land you want for nothing." And they were goin' to come the next summer and see me and I was goin' to guide them to a place where they could settle down. I knew all that country in there.

But that winter when they got back to Edmonton, they stayed in a hotel quite a while, him and her. He figured he didn't have enough money, so he thought he'd go way back up the Nahanni River to trap again and get some more fur. He started out and he left her there. That was the last that was seen of him.

A search party went after him and sixty miles up the Nahanni River they found the remains of a camp and there was a wooden post in the centre of the remains. The camp had been burned down. I guess it was the Indians that did it. There was a post right there in the centre of the ashes: "William Power *fini*." It was cut into the post. That was the last I heard of him and her. The Indians probably thought he was goin' to steal their furs, like the Mad Trapper.


I was with Henry on two trips up there. I brought some samples out and the mining engineers come in and we had to take another trip up there. It was a hard trip, took us six days to get in, walkin' over the tundra, broken rocks and streams and everything else, to get into this big limestone mountain. They used to call it White Mountain. The deposit I found was up there 2,000 feet, the Richardson Range northwest of Aklavik. They brought us in on the plane and left us there.

You'd work up all day on this mountain where Henry and I were strippin' off this talus to get this thing exposed. We'd work there for two or three hours 'til you get down to the frost and then you couldn't dig anymore and you'd have to come down and go home. Make supper and then you'd have three hours' sleep and you were just as fresh as though you were sleepin' for a week. Then you'd get up and take a rifle and go off in the middle of the night way down the old riverbed and shoot grizzlies.

There was one time we came out of the mountains to Aklavik at the end of a season and we were waitin' for the steamboat to come down to bring us back home, back out to Fort McMurray.

There was an old lady used to come in there with her beautiful, big son. They were all dressed in furs and they had a beautiful schooner there. She used to come in and Henry and I got to talkin' to her (Henry could talk Eskimo pretty good). He found out that this boy's father was an explorer—what's his name, a Swedish name—and he promised to take this son out to civilization to get educated. Stefanssen, that was his name.

Stefanssen came out to civilization and he was lecturin' all over the States and Canada but he never went back to get that son. And she used to come in there every summer, the boy and her, to sell their winter's catch of white fox. And she used to walk up and down in front of the Hudson Bay post lookin' for Steffansen and she was disappointed every summer. She did that for five or six summers.

So Henry got to talkin' to her and she said, "Come on aboard this afternoon and we'll have a little talk, a cup of tea." Henry and I went over and got on the schooner. They had great big drums there, those ornery big oil drums with the top cut out of them. They had two of them on board there. And she come out with a galvanized pail full of tea. Darn weak tea, too. They just put a pinch in a pail of water.

Then she went over with two tin cups and went to this barrel and scooped out a cupful of the stuff and gave us both a cup. Henry looked at me and said, "Don't touch it." Just like that. I knew he wasn't goin' to drink it, but she started talkin' Eskimo to him and she was insulted.

You know what it was? In the spring, they kill these baby seals and they put them in these barrels and let them rot and ferment and then the oil out of the seal would come to the top and the sediment would settle. Then they used to dish up this stuff and drink it down. It was supposed to be a delicacy.

Henry put it to his lips, took one sip of it and put it down. I took a shot of it too and pretty near threw up my insides. However, it had to be done to satisfy her. We never drank any more but we drank all the bloomin' tea we could get into us, so-called tea. Coloured water. But they were satisfied.

Then they brought us down in the bow of the boat and these two (this son and the old girl had over $15,000 in the bank in Edmonton) and they had a big locker across and inside was kind of a cold storage with the whole place packed solid with white fox pelts. White fox pelts when I was up there were worth $50 apiece. Every summer she'd come in and sell so much to the Hudson Bay, then she'd fill the locker up again that winter and sell some more and send the money through the Hudson Bay post down to the bank in Edmonton.

There was a small, little Hudson Bay outpost, a little cabin, it wouldn't be more than twelve feet square.

They had one of these scions of some rich family over in Scotland there. He was a nice fellow, his name was Clark, big, fair fella. Spoke Scotch. They put him in charge. That's the way the Hudson Bay people do. They get hold of these rich guys in the old country, these fellas that are useless over there and their parents don't know what to do with them. If they get them a job with the Honourable Hudson Bay Company of Adventurers, they're tickled all to hell to get out in the wilds.

So Clark was one of them. He had lots of money. Well-educated, he'd be about twenty-two. And the Hudson Bay dumped him way back there in this little cabin and there was one Eskimo family in that whole region, just one family. There was two boys, the old man and the old lady.

Ernie and I were there for about a week right in the middle of fly time. All we had was the tent. We couldn't stay in the little cabin with Clark 'cause there wasn't room. He had a few shelves with some red cloth, beads and some tobacco and tea, mostly tea.

One other time up there, I and my partner, a fellow by the name of Ernie Rivers, (I met him again this summer when I was prospectin' in Shining Tree) well, Ernie and I were shipped up to Hudson Bay and then they took us inland about two hundred miles on the west shore. They dumped us off there to prospect. We had about a ton of grub with us and lots of supplies. Dumped us at the head of a long lake.

And this little cabin was all built out of little poles the size of your wrist, that's the biggest timber they had up in that country, all twisted and gnarled and plastered up with frozen mud.

So we were in the tent. We had a cheesecloth front to it and the mosquitoes were so thick outside that tent you could just grab the tent from the inside and it would be just a ball of mush. They were about two inches thick. You could hardly see fer the bloomin' things. We used to run from the tent to get in the shack.

There was one day in there I said to myself, what are we goin' to do? I asked Ernie, "Have you got any raisins here?" He says, "Sure." I said, "Let's set a brew. Get somethin' to drink."

We had no rum, no liquor. So we got two quart jars and I set them and made a brew. In a couple of days it was pretty strong and we got pretty tight. I got to thinkin' we should give this Eskimo family a shot of it and see what they'd do.

The big, wide creek was all openin' up in the spring, big chunks of ice comin' down. Well, we give them a shot or two of that apiece and by god, they just went clean wild. They stripped off stark naked and they got in that ice-cold water, jumpin' from one iceberg to another and rollin' in the water. They had a heck of a time.

So that night they calmed down but they wanted some more. We had no more to give them—they drank the full quart. That night we were back in the tent and we heard the drums goin' bang, bang, bang. Ernie says to me, "What are they celebratin' now? They're all over their booze." We didn't know and waited 'til the mornin'.

George Clark comes in and says the old man died last night. "We're goin' to bury him. You better come to the funeral and see how it goes." The family was all lined up. They had this big caribou skin and they had the old man inside it, all sewn up. He was right inside there, stretched right out with a rope on him and they were draggin' him off into the bush, where they'd pile the stones around him.

And there was another fella behind, he had a sleigh and he was draggin' the sleigh with the old man's traps, his rifle, two or three pots and pans, some old pieces of bone knives, all his belongings.

Ernie and I were taggin' on right behind the old man when they were draggin' him. And by god, I saw the old man's knee come up inside the bag. I said, "George! He's alive." George says, "Like hell he is." I says, "Look at his knee. It's movin'."

George stopped the procession right away, ripped open the bag. The old fella stretched himself, stood up on his legs and there was big rejoicin'. They went back to the tent and they had a big celebration. The powwows was goin', the drums were goin' and they were yellin' and havin' a great time.

But the old fella did die that next mornin'. He died, sure enough, and they had the same thing the next day. He never pulled up a knee that mornin'.

And they brought him down, stretched him out and piled all the stones over top of him there, chinked all the holes with moss. Then took all his belongings, his frying pan and his traps, and put them on top of the pile of stones.

You know, all these Eskimos have a little telescope about that long, so they can look and see when the caribou are comin' over the ridges. Since we didn't have a pair of binoculars with us or nothin',

Ernie and I, I took a fancy with that old Eskimo's telescope and I was goin' to get it.

As soon as the funeral was over I sneaked back and grabbed the telescope off of the grave, stuck it in my pocket. I looked through it two or three times but you could hardly see anything. The lens was all scratched up. But, however, I kept it anyway.

We got into George's place, the little cabin, the next day and the old Eskimo's wife had been in there two or three times. There was somethin' goin' on. I went in anyway.

George says to me, "Look it here. What have you been up to?"

I says, "Sawin'. Are we goin' to make some more brew?"

"No," he says, "no more beer, no more brew. I have no more raisins."

I said, "What's wrong?"

He said, "You stole a telescope off that grave." I denied it for a while, you know, and he knew that I did.

"Now," he says, "there's no use in foolin', you have that telescope."

"Yah," I said, "I have it."

"Well, for godsakes go and put it back or you'll be chased out of the country. Maybe they'll shoot you."

I says, "You're kiddin'."

"No."

I was sittin' in the corner of the shack and Clark was behind the counter. Then in came the old girl with a great big knife as long as your arm in one hand and a frying pan in the other. She had a great big lump on her shoulder as big as a grapefruit. I thought it was full of pus or a big ulcer or some damn thing.

She came in the door and she came over to me and she was goin' to slash me on the top of the head and George let a roar out of him and she stopped. Then she talked in Eskimo to him for quite a while. Finally, she went out. George said, "That's what you're goin' to get." I said I'd put it back.

"That'll help but it's not the best. You've disturbed that where they've put it." They figure the Supreme Bein' was goin' to come back and get all that stuff, the traps, the pan and the telescope, and everything would be all right.

(They used to go there every mornin' and put some bannock in the old frying pan and the foxes used to come and steal it out of the pan and the Eskimos thought it was the spirits gettin' it.)

Well, the old wife came in another day and I was sittin' in the same place and she come in with that big knife just the same. And she was talking away (I don't know what she was sayin'), but George got her calmed down. He took a big bolt of red cloth off the shelf and cut her off two or three yards, gave her some tea and some tobacco and away she went. Everything was quietened down.

I says to George, "Look it here, what about that big lump on her shoulder? I can fix that. Have you got any razor blades?" "Sure", says George. So he called her in and he had a long talk with her. Told her that I was a medicine man. Oh, she believed it, and she was goin' to get it done the next mornin'. She came along the next day and bared her shoulder and it was just like a big coconut stuck there. I got out the razor blade and the minute she saw the razor she took off. I never saw her again.


There was one time at Padlei, that's at the Hudson Bay post there, we ran out of grub, gave all our grub to the Eskimos 'cause we knew darn well the plane would bring us in tons more.

But this time we ran out. The plane came in to see how we were gettin' along, get our notes and samples. I says we're pretty near out of grub. Some of us got to go out to the base camp, fly back and pick out what grub we want, bring it back in again. So Ernie and I drew straws to see who'd go. And he drew the longest straw and he went out with the plane.

When he got to base camp he was there two days and he got arthritis or rheumatism. This was all a put-up game, he just didn't want to go back to the flies. He was there two weeks and I was all alone with nothin' to eat and no sign of him comin'.

I stayed there four or five days and then I thought well, there's an Eskimo family 'bout nine mile down the lake. They had some old canoes there, all battered up but they'd still float. I thought if I went there I could get a canoe, then go through to the coast, 150 miles down this river, and reach base camp. So I went down and stayed with the Eskimos one night. I got up the next mornin' and I was crawlin' with lice from head to foot, great big jiggers, as big as a grain of rice.

I didn't know too much Eskimo but I made signs. There was a pretty smart fellow there and he could talk a small bit of English and he understood me. I told him I'd give him the value of two white foxes from the Hudson Bay Company fer this old canoe. He was satisfied. He made me out a map where I had to go 60 miles down the rapids, then straight across the lake and I'd hit the mouth of the big river and I'd get clean sailin' from there down. He told me there were rock piles along the way and what the shape of each rock pile meant, danger places and sharp curves, where different things had been killed, a kind of history all the way down.

I couldn't read the bloomin' rocks. His talk just went in one side of my head and out the other. I set off in the canoe with my eiderdown and a little piece of tobacco. No grub. I had a fishin' line. I thought I could go down in a couple of days. Tough goin' but I'd make it all right 'cause the water was swift.

I paddled ten miles down the rapids and I had to make a short bend. I saw this big pile of rocks on the right side and I knew it meant somethin' 'cause it was way bigger than any other pile, but I didn't have time to think. I just turned round the bend and I was right on top of the falls. There were three steps to the falls. You'd go down ten feet, you'd go along a little piece, then go down ten feet, like a great big set of stairs.

I jumped them all right. I was pretty good in a canoe, went right down through the centre and took in 'bout a pail of water. The old canoe was spongey, the bottom heavin' up and down, the cedar was all cracked. But I made right down to Lake Kazan. I looked across and it was all tall reeds and you couldn't find the mouth of the river. I paddled up and down lookin' fer it and I couldn't even find a current.

Well, I thought it must be way down the end of the lake 'bout twenty miles. I paddled down but still no outlet and came back where I'd first come out and camped on a rock. I had a big magnifying glass with me.

Waited 'til a real nice day and I gathered up a whole bunch of this caribou moss (it's just like celluloid, put a match to it and it'll flare up). I got pulp out of some old dead wood and I had a nice pile there in case the plane would come along and I could make smoke.

And I was catchin' trout. You could catch trout just over the side of the canoe. Just drop your hook in the water with a piece of any-thing, a button, and you'd have a beautiful trout that long. I had no salt but I used to cook the trout sometimes when I could get the glass workin' on a bright day, half-cook it. I ate raw fish there fer 'bout two weeks. Got used to it, wasn't nourishin' but kept me from starvin'.

The old eiderdown was soggy and heavy. The old canoe, I pulled it up on the bank and turned it upside down. I was there 'bout two weeks, just didn't know what to do, how to get out of there, couldn't find the mouth of the river. I wasn't goin' to carry the canoe over the rocks that distance, 150 miles.

All of a sudden I heard a plane way south. They were goin' way up to where I'd started from, where Ernie had left me, to see if I was there. Well, I wasn't. They followed the river down, sure enough, they come over to where I was and I had the smoke goin'. That bloomin' plane, there was lots of water fer them to land on and they had pontoons. They circled me three or four times and took off. Never said a word. They made no signs or nothin'.

I thought they musta brought Ernie in and I'd better start working upstream again. So I did that. I went up through the rapids, wading water for two weeks, fightin' rapids all the way, mosquitoes and every bloomin' thing. All I could feed on was the raw trout. I'd lost an awful lot of weight.

I was just breakin' over the head of the rapids and gettin' into smooth water when I met Ernie comin' down with two Eskimos in a canoe. I waved them to stop. My god, he didn't know me, I'd faded that much. I was just skin and bones.

He was glad to see me and he had a whole bunch of grub, but I was too weak to eat. He gave me a glass of rum and I passed out.


There was another time (this was 1929 just before we were told to pull up stakes and get out of the country) we were way down the Camsell River, went down by canoe and landed, put up our tent and we were goin' to start prospectin'.

A little canoe come along with a boy in it, a young girl, her father and an old lady, and they landed on the shore. After a while the father, he came up to the tent and he was cryin', makin' signs, we didn't know what the dickens he was sayin', cryin' and pointin' to the shore. So Ernie and I went down and the old lady was layin' there on some moss. The boy and girl both cryin'. They thought she was ready to die. They wanted to try and save her.

Ernie says to me, "You can't do anything with her. They're different people. You don't know the nature of their blood." I says, "I'll fix her." I had a bottle of Perry Davis pain killer. It's kind of a liniment you can take inwards and outwards and it burns the life right outa you. I poured some of that into a dish and went down to her.

I thought she had pneumonia. But I got her mouth open with a chunk of stick and I poured that stuff in her, guzzled her throat and got it down into her. By god, in fifteen minutes she was right up, she was all right, come right to. Musta had gas in her stomach. She was all bloated up. They were celebratin' then, makin' tea, smokin', and dancin' around.

Then Bill Spence came in with the plane and landed there. He never brought any supplies or nothin' and I says, "What are you in fer?" He said, "You can just take your belongings, leave all the rest of your stuff. The world market, the outfit is all crashed, they're finished, everything is finished." So he gave us what he heard over the radio 'bout the big market crash. We just took our eiderdown, our shaving outfit and left the tent there and maybe fifteen hundred pounds of all kinds of groceries, bacon and canned stuff.

So that Eskimo family was all set for a while. Bet she got a belly-ache after eatin' all that stuff!


I'm goin' to tell you something that gotta be kept fairly secret. At the time of this big depression, when everybody was pretty near starvin' up in this country, heck, the poor farmer, he had to go out and dig ditches there in the snow in the middle of winter and summer. He could only get work maybe for two days a week at a dollar and a half a day. There were real hard times. Well, I didn't do it. I didn't do any digging. I used to make whiskey and sell it for five dollars a bottle. I made hundreds of gallons and I prospered all right.

The Mounties were after me and the provincial police, but I was too smart for them to get me, too good in the bush. I'd have a great big still set back in the bush with three or four barrels of brew and I'd run the thing off. If I got wind of somebody comin' along, I'd get up in the middle of the night and pack the stuff to another creek miles away. Not go over the same place twice.

There was one time I had three big barrels of mash set close to a creek and it was all ready to run. I went back this day and I had a rifle with me, always carried a rifle. And here the three big barrels were upset. It was a corn mash that I had in there and here was four bears so drunk they couldn't move. They were layin' there, drunk, and I just put a bullet through each of their heads and that was it. I lost 200 pounds of sugar, 50 pounds of corn and all my trouble sterilizing the barrels, and those three sons of guns got the whole works.

I was up Long Lac one time and the little baby and the wife was there. She was a great musician, a wonderful piano player. She was always playing that great big Steinway concert piano we had in the front room. And I was trappin' up there that winter. It was against the law, contraband. Everything was closed out. But I'd got this great big beaver skin, squared about 82 inches, a record, and I didn't know where to hide it. So I opened the front of the piano down, shut the beaver skin in on top of the wires and put the thing back up.

Now I was down the lake 'bout three miles that same afternoon givin' a fellow a hand to take some logs out of the bush. A young lad come up from further down the lake and told us there were two provincial men on the portage, shootin' rabbits. I knew darn well that was no place for provincial men. They must be after something. So I put on my snowshoes and hied back home. I had this great big still in the back shed and there'd been a fresh fall of snow, so I knew I couldn't take the still out to the bush 'cause I'd leave snowshoe tracks. They'd find it easily. I puzzled my brains. From the lake up to the house was about 100 yards and there was pretty near close to three feet of snow. I used to go down and carry up the water and the trail was pretty well packed. I took the shovel and went right down the trail 'til halfway, then I dug the snow carefully and put the still down there, put the snow back on, circled snow that I had in the packsack and sprinkled it around the house. Just left a smooth trail. The copper can wasn't that far under the snow and if you tramped really hard you could hear the hollow sound. But I had to take a chance and do something.

So I went to bed 'bout two o'clock in the morning. A team of horses drove up and two policemen rapped at the door. There was a game warden with them, too. So I got up. Come on in, come on in. On a clothesline in front of the wood stove, I had a beaver castor dryin', pretty fresh 'cause they were out of that big beaver. Anyway, in they came and they were all white with frost and pretty near frozen.

The minute the game warden come in, he saw those castors hangin' there and he made a grab for them and I says, "Hold on! You can't touch those, they're mine. I got those from an Indian and I'm goin' to make medicine out of them." You can dissolve a beaver castor in alcohol and it's awfully good stuff if you got a sore back or sore kidneys. But he wouldn't believe it; they'd had a few shots of liquor on the way up, pretty snappy. He stuck the castors in his pocket and he said he was goin' to pinch me for havin' them.

And I had a big barrel of mash I set about two days ago right behind the stove. This constable says, "What have you got in that barrel?" I says, "A little homemade wine." He tasted it and said, "By god, that's pretty strong wine. Where's your still?" I says, "Who told you I had one?" Then he said, "Who plays the piano?" I said, "The wife does." She was still in bed behind the curtain and Ruth, the baby, was layin' along aside of her. "I play a little myself. Do you mind if I play a tune?" he asked.

And I'd been making pancakes, scones and coffee for them on the stove and I says go ahead. He gets on the piano and strikes a few chords and the keys were rapping up against this damn beaver skin. He says, "What in hell's wrong with this thing? You don't play on this do you?" I says yah. He looked around. He was pretty cute. He said there was something wrong with those keys. I knew I was dished then. He pulls the front of the piano down and pulls out the great big beaver skin. And the game warden right there. Well, he was right in his glory and he had me right there with a $50 fine.

And the constable says he was sent up to pinch me for making whiskey. He said, "Go out and get me a bottle, 'cause I've got to take this stuff down to get tests for analysis to see how much alcohol is in it." I had some empty bottles in the shed at the back and I poured some coal oil into one and took it back. The constable takes the bottle and shoves it down into the brew and gets it about three-quarters full of brew. Puts the cork in and gets it into his pocket. That's all the evidence they could get. He said I'd have to go to court and serve the summons. So I made about five trips down to Englehart with no result. They couldn't do anything. I had to pay a fine for the beaver skin, but they couldn't catch me on the liquor 'cause the coal oil spoiled all the investigation down there.

And the minute they left the house the next morning, I was scared stiff but I kept calm. Now mind you, they went from the house to the waterhole three or four times and they were walkin' over the still, right underneath their snowshoes. If they'd have gone along that trail and punched down with an iron rod, but they didn't know enough to do that. There was no tracks round the house, just fresh snow, and they thought that was all there was.

Soon as they left, I took the barrel of brew out and put it on a toboggan, took it clean across the lake and shoveled away the snow and put that barrel of brew down there. It had to work three more days before I could distil it. Not strong enough. I covered it up with snow to create its own heat and by god, in three days I ran the whole thing off. Fifteen gallons and I sold the whole works for five dollars a quart. I used to bring it down to the dances, three and four gallons. The wife would play the piano down at the school and I'd play the violin and I'd be peddlin' whiskey on the side.

There was another time I was bringin' two gallons over to Elk Lake for to sell. The old wooden bridge was there then and I came over in a Model T Ford, I and another fellow from Charlton. The road was just barely a trail and the old Model T was just jumpin' along and I had these gallons of high wines. We'd stop on the far side of the town first. There was a Chinee there, an old Chinee. He had a restaurant and I heard he was a bootlegger. I went into him and he couldn't talk English very good. "Oh me don' know, me don' know. Me have lots whiskey, me no buy. How much?" I said, "Fifteen dollars a gallon."

He tasted it and said, "Pretty good lick, pretty good lick." Then he got one of those damn squares with all these beads on it and he started shufflin' the beads back and forth. I says, "What the hell are you doin' with that?" "Oh me get the bill. Me give you seventeen dollars for both cans." I said, "No good. Where else can I sell it?" He said, "Maybe Ethel Snider."

She had kind of a blind pig there and she used to keep a couple of girls there on the other side of town. So I said to Tommy, the fellow who was with me in the Model T, "We'll drive across the bridge. You stop there and don't drive any further. I'll take these two cans to Ethel Snider's through the bush." So I did that and he stayed at the bridge.

I went up to old Ethel. She'd just bought a shipment the night before and she said she couldn't handle any more. So I said "What am I goin' to do with them now? Supposin' I leave them here, you can pay me some other time." "No," she says, "they can search there any old time."

Then a young kid came in from downtown. "Is that your Model T down there? The police are searchin' all through it." I says, "Nope, that's not mine." I told Ethel I gotta take the stuff out and there was a river near. She gave me a piece of rope, tied it round the two cans and put it round my neck. I jumped in the river and swam across. Tom met me in the car about a quarter mile outside of town. The police couldn't find anything. And then we started back to Charlton with these two cans and got four miles outside Elk Lake. Along come the police with a car behind. Remember the old Model T, there was a little, small window in the back. Well, this window was broken and I had a .22 rifle in the car. "Tommy," I says, "take the wheel quick." And I got the twenty-two and just when they got within shootin' distance I pumped five shots into their front tires. Pinned them right there and we kept on goin'. Got back to Charlton with the two cans.


I went to Gowganda and took up trappin'. I got a cabin and took a partner in with me and I got four husky dogs. Archie Peever and I used to go down the lakes one day and come back the next, gather up all the beaver out of the traps, then skin for two or three days, and then come to town for Saturday, Sunday and Monday and get drunk. In two months Archie and I made $4,000 in fur. We were gettin' the choice of the skins because they were old beaver and the skins were large, pretty near half the size of that table. We used to get $90 a pelt but the next year, it all went flop. Skins went down to nothing.

I remarried about that time. She was a Roman Catholic and I wasn't. I don't believe in any of that nonsense. She'd turned anyway and we were married up in Timmins. One day she had to go and see the doctor in Kirkland Lake about something. I didn't know what. We were only married about two or three months. Anyway, she went and I gave her $160. She came back broke, not a nickel. Seems she got into a party with her sister; she loved her booze.

Then she had to see the doctor again about something. I don't know what he told her, but she came home. Never told me anything about it. I wasn't very inquisitive. But she was upstairs here one day. I'd just bought this place out of beaver skins. It was getting near suppertime. Frank Tibbs, the fire ranger, came by and sat down in that corner. She set the table, put the food out. Then she said she didn't feel like eatin'. Thought she'd go upstairs and lay down awhile. Frank and I kept on eating. Three or four days before, I was out in the shed. I had a bottle of strychnine to poison wolves, nobody was supposed to know I had the stuff, but she'd been nosin' around in there and saw this bottle and she asked me how much strychnine would it take to kill a wolf. "Oh," I said, "about the size of a bean. Just put it in a little lard and throw it in a carcass, for bait."

However, she had this in her mind and all of a sudden we heard moanin' and groanin'. I rushed upstairs and she was on the bed having a fit, frothing at the mouth. I hollered to Frank, "Come here." He said, "What's wrong? Epilepsy?" "No," I said, "she's got that damn strychnine." Well, Frank's wife came up and we beat her and slapped her and tried to stick something down her throat. She stiffed up and passed out. That was it.

Afterwards I found out what was botherin' her. I didn't know. She had cancer of the breast and the doctor told her it was too far gone. There was no cure. I guess that worked on her mind. She never told me anything at all. So that was the second wife gone. I've had bad luck with women.

# Alf Page
## Near Gowganda

Inside the cabin:

wood stove
five outdated calendars
1907 T. Eaton clock
two sofas
blue-flowered plastic curtains
two chipmunks
a wife
a radio

Lovely god, oh my gosh, the socials—better than it is now, oh yes. We had our dances and our picnics and every little thing that went on we was there. Better times in them days than there is now. The people aren't here, the ones that enjoyed that kind of life are gone.

People's that never lived here can't understand what keeps a person here. I went south once and got so damned homesick I couldn't stand it. I had to come back. I missed them loons flyin' overhead, oh yi, yi, yi.

I was my own boss trappin'. Once a guy starts trappin' he generally sticks to it. It's not a good life but he can make a livin' at it. But now, we live on pension. I mostly do tinkerin'. I read. Westerns. I know there's a lot of bull about them but it passes the time. Mum can't read. Her eyes are gone.

Our friends are goin' pretty fast now. We lost one just a couple of weeks ago. All the old fellas, all gone but two or three.

# The Haymaker

"Never be lost in the bush. All you got to do is watch the hay-maker up above. Sometimes the bark on a tree will tell you which way is north and which way is south. There's a little different colour. If you're lost and you come to a stream, watch which way that stream is runnin'. You follow it down and you're bound to get into high water. You'll come to a river and then a lake and you'll know where you are."